RAILS THR[O] WEXFORD

THE NORTH AND SOUTH WEXFORD LINES IN COLOUR

JONATHAN BEAUMONT AND BARRY CARSE

COLOURPOINT

Published 2023 by Colourpoint Books
an imprint of Colourpoint Creative Ltd
Colourpoint House, Jubilee Business Park
21 Jubilee Road, Newtownards, BT23 4YH
Tel: 028 9182 6339
E-mail: sales@colourpoint.co.uk
Web: www.colourpoint.co.uk

First Edition
First Impression

A catalogue record for this book is available from the British Library.

Designed by April Sky Design, Newtownards
Tel: 028 9182 7195
Web: www.aprilsky.co.uk

Printed by GPS Colour Graphics Ltd, Belfast
ISBN 978-1-78073-381-4

About the authors: Jonathan Beaumont and Barry Carse are both lifelong railway enthusiasts who have an extensive knowledge of the railways of Ireland. Jonathan Beaumont has previously published *Rails to Achill: A West of Ireland Branch Line (*Oakwood Press, *2002), Achillbeg: The Life of an Island* (Oakwood Press, 2005) and *Rails Through Connemara: The Galway-Clifden Railway* (Oakwood Press, 2021) as well as many articles. Barry Carse is a well known and accomplished railway photographer with an extensive collection of images from across Ireland. He has previously published *Irish Metro-Vick Diesels* (Colourpoint Books, 1997) as well as numerous articles in the IRRS Journal. Together they published *Rails Through The West: An illustrated journey on the Western Rail Corridor* (Colourpoint Books, 2012), *Rails Through North Kerry: Limerick to Tralee and Branches* (Colourpoint Books, 2016) and *Rails Through Tipperary: Limerick to Waterford* (Colourpoint Books, 2021).

We dedicate this book to the railway
staff who worked on the lines featured.

CONTENTS

INTRODUCTION

The two railway lines which crossed the southern part of County Wexford were of considerable interest to the railway enthusiast as well as the travelling public, yet both were opened towards the very end of the railway building era. The Dublin & South Eastern Railway had reached Wexford in 1872 and New Ross in 1887, with Rosslare being connected to Wexford in 1882. However what would later become known as the North Wexford and South Wexford lines would not open until the early years of the 20th century.

While the section from Macmine Junction to New Ross had been opened in 1887, the gap between the latter and Waterford was not bridged until 1904. The direct Waterford–Rosslare Strand route did not commence operations until even later in 1906, and was primarily built to speed transit from Rosslare Harbour to points south and west. While it did not pass through any sizeable settlement en route, this line had the prestigious 'Rosslare Express' which operated daily in each direction between Rosslare, Waterford, Mallow and Cork.

Both lines settled down into a somewhat different style of operation between their opening and the early 1960s. While the south line had the Rosslare Express, other traffic was sparse, and was typically served by two passenger trains per day, plus a goods train. These operated from Waterford through to Rosslare Harbour, although between 1906 and 1911 there was a spur at Felthouse Junction (see map) allowing trains to traverse this line and head north to Wexford without reversing at Rosslare Strand.

Once the north line was opened from New Ross into Waterford, the Dublin & South Eastern Railway (DSER) was able to operate a through service from Dublin to Waterford, competing with the Great Southern & Western Railway whose line entered Waterford from the Kilkenny direction. The new DSER service involved splitting the down train at Macmine Junction. One portion continued to Wexford. The other portion – including the dining car – travelled via the branch to Waterford.

In later years, however, when both companies were amalgamated into the Great Southern Railways, the North Wexford line was treated like a backwater with only a local train service.

By the dawn of the 1960s, these lines were part of the nationalised system of Córas Iompair Eireann. As a result of the retrenchment and modernisation programme in the late 1950s and early 1960s, the passenger train service was withdrawn from the north line, and the original section of it from Macmine Junction to New Ross closed completely in 1963 with the tracks removed soon afterwards. This left just the New Ross–Waterford section which remained open to general goods traffic until 3 September 1976. After that, only fertiliser and cement traffic was handled, but this ceased operating in 1995. The line remained dormant, gradually becoming more overgrown and eventually impassable. Nature encroached, as occasionally did landowners adjacent to the line, but it was not until some years later that the line was formally abandoned. Since then, it has been converted into a cycleway. New Ross station itself had been levelled while still carrying bulk freight, as the old passenger platforms, signal cabin and buildings were no longer needed.

Meanwhile, the south line continued in operation but with little interest shown by the railway authorities in developing traffic along it, goods traffic dwindled and the passenger service was reduced to but one or two trains per day, increasingly at times of no use to local people who might wish to travel into Waterford for the day. By this time all stations were not only unstaffed, but even the buildings had been cleared away except at Wellington Bridge and Rosslare Strand where the line joined the Rosslare–Wexford–Dublin line. The very few prospective passengers had only a rudimentary bus shelter in which to await their train. Hardly surprising, the train service was suspended in 2010. Iarnród Eireann continued to operate a weedspraying train occasionally for some years afterwards, the last time being on 31 May 2022, when Multi-Purpose Vehicle No 790 traversed the line.

Why, one might wonder, did the south line even last as long as it did? While it gave connections to and from ferries from Rosslare to Wales at one time, in the final years any pretence of doing so had been long abandoned. If either line was to be retained, why not the northern route, as it served the sizeable town of New Ross?

The reason was that the South Wexford area was, until 2006, one of Ireland's main areas of production of sugar beet, and this cargo was shipped in huge quantities to the sugar factory at Mallow, Co Cork. At one time, sugar beet had been sent from points of origin all over Ireland to factories at Carlow, Thurles, Tuam and Mallow. By the turn of the 21st century only the latter remained, but large quantities of beet were still travelling from Co Wexford. By degrees, smaller loading points were abandoned and loading into trains was concentrated at Wellington Bridge on the south Wexford. It is hardly surprising, then, that once this traffic ceased as a result of changes in government agricultural subsidies, the entire line lost all services and the Barrow Bridge fell into disuse.

The importance of the sugar beet industry to the area cannot be overstated, and the exceptionally heavy rail traffic as a result of it is given a feature of its own in this book, which aims to show the character of both lines from the photographs of Barry Carse. In the case of the North Wexford line, the New Ross to Macmine Junction was closed sufficiently early to be outside the remit of this photographic collection, and few other photographers visited it. Thus, the authors have utilised images from other sources to cover this section.

Today, the only line in this area is the stretch from Rosslare Harbour to Wexford and onwards to Dublin. There are four trains per day between Rosslare Europort and Wexford, and onwards towards Dublin, at the time of writing in 2023.

Jonathan Beaumont
Barry Carse
April 2023

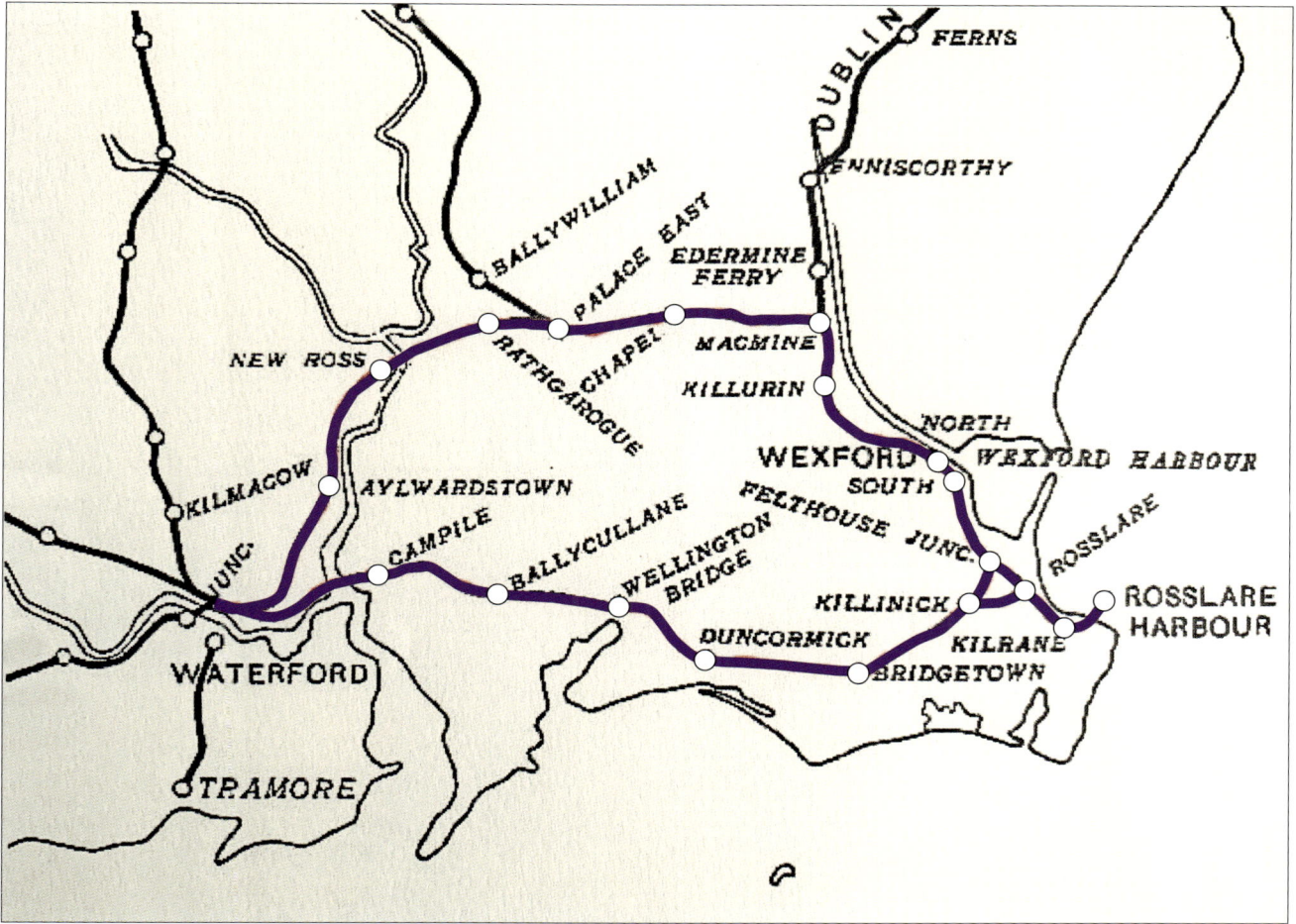

A map of the routes covered in this book.

THE NORTH WEXFORD LINE

The North Wexford line was opened in 1906, following the extension of the Dublin, Wicklow & Wexford Railway from Macmine Junction and Palace East to New Ross, with a final extension into Waterford. Upon opening this section, it became renamed as the Dublin & South Eastern Railway. Waterford station was operated by the Great Southern & Western Railway, and the DSER now had permission to operate into it. The entire route lost its passenger service from 1 April 1963, with the section between New Ross and Macmine Junction being closed entirely from the same date and later dismantled. The section from New Ross had a daily goods train until 1976, and was closed entirely in 1995 following its last few years of being used only for fertiliser and bagged cement traffic. Today, parts of this line are in use as a cycleway.

Locomotive B166 pictured at Waterford on a train for Macmine Junction on 28 March 1963, a few days before closure of the New Ross–Macmine Junction section with effect from 1 April. *(Roger Joanes)*

Crossley-engined locomotive No C216 pauses at Waterford, in the former Rosslare bay platform, mid-1960s. By this time a locomotive inspection pit had been added here as this place was used for stabling locomotives. *(Colour-Rail)*

B121 class No B135 has just arrived from Macmine Junction at Waterford on 27 March 1963, four days before this service was withdrawn *(Roger Joanes)*

Following closure to passengers in 1963, the line between Waterford and New Ross was used only for goods trains for some years afterwards, as mentioned above. Here, locomotive B103 is seen at Waterford with the New Ross goods of just one empty open wagon, 1969 – normally, this train was a great deal busier! The old Rosslare bay platform is seen to the left, disused since the early 1960s. *(Roger Joanes)*

Locomotive 186 passes Abbey Junction on its way into Waterford from New Ross on 11 August 1973. The locomotive is in the newly introduced 'Supertrain' livery. The train has brought peat moss from Coolnamona, outside Portlaoise to New Ross for export. This operation involved the train leaving the siding at Coolnamona, on the stub of the erstwhile Portlaoise–Kilkenny line; travelling to Kildare, then Kilkenny, and having to change direction at each of those locations. Onwards to Waterford, and up the branch to New Ross.

A train of empty cement wagons approaches Waterford from New Ross on 24 October 1980. The train arrived with five wagons, but another fifteen were added in Waterford before the train proceeded to Limerick. The locomotive was No 003. The former Ardree Hotel towers over the station on the right.

Locomotive 165 hauls four laden fertiliser wagons from New Ross towards Waterford on 30 January 1995. The train is destined for Mallow. With newly upgraded track, this stretch of line was just north of Abbey Junction. This portion of track had recently been lowered to facilitate the construction of an overbridge to provide access to Belview Port.

B101 class No B112 heads towards Glenmore with the 08:00 goods train to New Ross on 6 August 1970. One goods van in the middle of the train bears the then-new brown livery for wagons. This train was running very late on this day because the locomotive had earlier operated a short passenger working with a single coach to the power station at Kilmokea, on the South Wexford Line. By this stage, appearances of locomotives of this class on passenger trains was becoming rare.

Glenmore, with a typical Dublin & South Eastern Railway building, on 24 July 1974. Locomotive 004 has a light load of just two goods vans and one Bell container, plus the obligatory brake van. The train has paused to facilitate the photographer, who had requested a journey over the line in the cab! The former down platform (on the right) is by now long disused. This station was originally known as 'Glenmore & Aylwardstown'.

On 15 August 1977, an 001 class locomotive heads a train of empty carriages to New Ross in the early morning light to form the 08:30 special train to Waterford (with a bus connection to Tramore). This was an excursion operation which took place on 15 August each year to mark the Feast of the Assumption. The train is made up of coaches of a number of designs, as was then typical. Behind the locomotive is a 'BR' steam generating van, followed by a 1955-built 'Park Royal' coach, then three late 1950s 'Laminates',

a 1963-built 'Craven' and finally a full brake van dating from the early 1950s. The location is in the townland of Carrickcloney, near Glenmore.

The same train returned to collect another trainload of people, and this departed from New Ross at 12:30. Here it is seen heading back into Waterford. Across the River Barrow on the right is Dunganstown, the ancestral home of the former American President John F Kennedy.

17

On 12 May 1979, the Irish Railway Record Society organised a tour in conjunction with the Locomotive Club of Great Britain, originating in Dublin and covering the New Ross line. The locomotives are 186 and 155, with kitchen car 2403, third vehicle behind the locomotives. Later in the day the two locomotives were replaced by B121 class Nos 129 and 134.

Seventeen days later, on 29 May 1979, one of the same locomotives, 186, is seen during its tour of the entire railway system with the annual weedspraying train. This train carried these distinctive striped warning signs for many years. The train is pictured near Glenmore.

Locomotive 004 leaves New Ross with a lightly loaded goods train for Waterford on 24 July 1974. It is pictured here approaching Staffords' Siding.

The same train is pictured shunting Staffords' Siding, New Ross, before it left with the goods train for Waterford. It picked up one wagon here with a Bell container.

The same level crossing after the line had fallen into disuse, in 1996. Following renewal of the road surface, a section of track had been replaced (by the road people!) on top of the original, instead of placed into it!

Locomotive 004 shunts New Ross station on 24 July 1974. Most of the original buildings are still intact, eleven years after the last regular passenger services ceased and the line forwards to Macmine Junction was closed. The agricultural equipment unloaded on the platform on the left is indicative of the wide variety of freight still handled by rail at this stage.

Locomotive 019 arrives very early in the morning at New Ross with empty carriages. The train will form the pilgrimage train to Knock for the Augustinian Order, on 12 September 1976. The train left New Ross at 07:45 for Waterford, where it connected with the 07:30 from Killinick which would take a lengthy route to Claremorris via Kilkenny and Kildare, in order to serve other Augustinian communities along its chosen route. 114 passengers joined in New Ross, another 106 in Waterford, and a further 79 in Kilkenny.

The same train awaits departure. It would proceed to Waterford where more carriages were added in the form of a separate train from the South Wexford Line. The combined train would then proceed to Claremorris. Many of these trains involved a very long day for participants, often not arriving back at their point of origin until after midnight.

'001' class locomotives were regulars on the Waterford–New Ross line in the 1970s and 1980s. Here, 022 awaits unloading its train of seven bagged cement wagons at New Ross on 23 October 1978. By this time a new cement store had been provided by CIÉ.

On 30 January 1995, locomotive 165 is at New Ross with empty fertiliser wagons. The load of bagged fertiliser awaits on the left.

B141 class No 165 passes Staffords' Siding, New Ross, with a laden fertiliser train on 13 January 1995.

On the same day, 121 class locomotives 121 and 129 arrive at New Ross with five empty fertiliser wagons in the afternoon. The maximum load allowed on the branch was equivalent to seven and a half laden wagons. On this day there were ten empty wagons delivered, so once laden they had to be taken back to Waterford in two separate trains – in this case No 165 with four, and this pair of 121 class locomotives with six. All of these loads were destined for Mallow.

The fork lift loads the same train. By this stage the track has been reduced to a simple run round loop.

The River Barrow Bridge, just north of New Ross station, which survived the closure of the line north of the town and remains in situ today. (Oliver Doyle)

On 1 September 1963, the North Wexford line was specially reopened six months after closure to accommodate six special trains of supporters for the All-Ireland Hurling Final between Waterford and Kilkenny in Croke Park, Dublin. These were hauled by brand-new B141 class locomotives, some double-headed. Here, B148 and B170 approach the Barrow Bridge with the last of these trains. (Norman J McAdams, © Irish Railway Record Society).

Near Rathgarogue, an unidentified B121 class locomotive passes with a service train from Waterford to Macmine Junction. These locomotives were introduced into traffic less than two years before the line closed. Thus, the picture dates from some time between mid-1961 and the end of March 1963. *(Norman J McAdams, © Irish Railway Record Society)*

J15 class No 125 has the 16:25 train from Macmine Junction to Waterford at Rathgarogue on 28 October 1961. This line was one of the last outposts of steam traction on CIÉ. On the left is the well-known railway enthusiast David Houston. *(Norman Foster)*

On 9 July 1960, Dublin railway enthusiast G R Mahon was aboard an Irish Railway Record Society special train from Dublin via the south-eastern main line, and Macmine Junction, to New Ross and Waterford. Here, he captures the view from the train as it approaches Palace East, the junction for the former GSWR line to Bagenalstown in Co Carlow. On the left, the site of the turntable is evident as well as a siding. The station building is on a central island platform. *(G R Mahon, © Irish Railway Record Society)*

On 23 March 1963, the view ahead from Palace East, looking west towards New Ross (left) and Bagenalstown (right), seen from a train. The train was hauled by J15 class 0-6-0 No 151. (Michael Costelloe, © Irish Railway Record Society)

View from the overbridge looking east, Palace East, 9 July 1960. (Graham Hoare, © Irish Railway Record Society)

General view, Palace East, showing the typical 'tin shed' architecture used on both the North and South Wexford lines, despite their origins with different railway companies. This view was taken on 17 December 1959. (Chris Gammell, © Irish Railway Record Society)

Palace East station in October 2021, by permission of the landowner. The station is now a private residence.

An empty sugar beet train pauses at Chapel station on 11 November 1961. The train left Carlow at 03:10 as special train BT40 (empty wagons) to Wexford. The locomotive is J15 class 0-6-0 No 172. (*Norman Foster*)

B121 class locomotive No B135 stops at Chapel station en route from Macmine Junction to Waterford on 27 March 1963, four days before the line closed for good. These locomotives were new, having only been introduced into traffic during 1961, so their tenure on this line was short. (*Roger Joanes*)

Empty beet wagons arrive at Macmine Junction en route for Wexford on 11 November 1961. This is the same train pictured on page 33. *(Norman Foster)*

B135 is seen with a Waterford train awaiting departure on 27 March 1963 at Macmine Junction. *(Roger Joanes)*

MACMINE JUNCTION TO ROSSLARE HARBOUR

This section was composed of the final stretch of the erstwhile DSER main line into Wexford, where it was joined in 1882 by the Waterford & Wexford Railway who constructed the line along Wexford Quays to Rosslare Harbour (renamed Kilrane in 1906) and a siding to Rosslare Pier (renamed Rosslare Harbour in 1906). The W&WR opened a station, South Wexford, at the Rosslare end of the quays on 1 October 1885. It was closed by the GSR in 1925 but reopened soon afterwards, finally closing on 7 March 1977. The W&WR was taken over by the Fishguard & Rosslare Railways & Harbours Company – a joint venture between the GSWR and Great Western Railway to develop a through route from London to Cork and Killarney. The line covered by this book, south from the former Macmine Junction, today forms the final stretch of the Dublin to Rosslare Europort line served by passenger trains only.

On 14 April 1984, all that was left at Macmine Junction was the footbridge, still wearing its old coat of CIÉ green paint, and the remains of the platforms, as the 13:30 Dublin (Connolly)– Rosslare Harbour train passes with locomotive 031. Today even these remains have long gone and the site is covered in bushes.

Locomotive 182 passes Killurin station, closed since 31 March 1964, on 11 September 1976 with a ballast train from Lisduff Quarry.

On an unspecified date in summer 1974, B152 powers alongside the River Slaney near Ferrycarrig, Co Wexford. The train is the 15:05 Dublin (Connolly) to Rosslare Harbour service.

In the same location in 1980, the now-preserved locomotive 039 is in charge of the Dublin–Wexford liner, including many of the 10ft containers which were introduced with Railplan '80, a final modernisation programme which resulted in the end of the operation of loose-coupled goods trains in Ireland.

Bagged cement was a major contributor to rail freight in the 1980s. Here, on 8 March 1980, no less than 20 empty wagons from Wexford are heading back to Platin, near Drogheda, behind locomotive 003.

No 027 and ten laden wagons form a Shelton Abbey–Waterford fertiliser special seen here passing Ferrycarrig, Co Wexford, on Saturday 24 August 1980. It was customary to see workings like this on Saturdays in the early 1980s.

Nos 172 and B145 bask in the evening sun on Bank Holiday Sunday 3 August 1975 at Wexford (North) station with a substantial train of nine carriages. This is the 18:40 from Rosslare Harbour to Dublin (Connolly). On the left, a number of sidings remain, along with the locomotive turntable and water tower. Many turntables remained well after the demise of steam traction, as the single-cabbed B121 class diesels needed to be turned if working singly.

Watched by two observers and a dog, a Northern Ireland Railways 80-class railcar set led by No 95, with No 96 at the far end, make up an Irish National Foresters' Club special train from Belfast to Wexford on another bank holiday weekend – Saturday 5 August 1978. The second last intermediate coach has two yellow stickers on the side – these read 'CityTrack', a short-lived NIR branding for local commuter services in the Belfast area. The train stabled here overnight, but failed the following morning when returning, and had to be hauled by B141 class locomotive No 156.

Locomotive 154 arrives in Wexford with the daily liner train on a sunny evening in the early 1980s. Apart from the wagon of Guinness at the front, all the containers are the 10ft type. Two of the containers carry an earlier grey livery.

The goods yard at Wexford, showing the still extensive track layout in 1998. Here, on 25 July, the down morning passenger train is seen in the distance on the left, while No 156 has arrived with a cargo of ten bagged cement wagons from Limerick, via Waterford and Rosslare Strand.

The Railway Preservation Society of Ireland (RPSI) operates trains using Irish Rail diesel locomotives as well as with its own preserved steam locomotives. On Friday 7 May 2010, No 081 is stabled in the new loop at Wexford to allow the northbound 12:55 train from Rosslare Europort to Dublin to pass. The carriages are the RPSI's Whitehead-based Mk 2 set.

No 182 slowly makes its way along the quayside at Wexford with the 12:40 Waterford to Wexford goods train in September 1975. The variety of wagons will be noted – loose-coupled goods trains were by now becoming rarer. The original timber framework underneath the railway line is clearly evident here. The entire area to the left of the train in the picture has now been infilled and is a pedestrianised promenade.

No 158 doubles up with a 121 class No 122 on the 09:32 morning Dublin (Connolly)–Rosslare Harbour passenger train on 26 May 1982 as it enters the harbour tramway. The goods shed is in the background on the right.

On 1 March 1980, the Crescent Bridge between Wexford (South) and Wexford (North) stations was in the progress of being renewed. Train services were terminated at Wexford (North) with bus transfers from there to Rosslare. Here, locomotive 156 is in charge of the Engineer's Dept. train to recover the old bridge parts while the Inchicore 35 ton crane aided by a road crane stand by to lift the new bridge into place. The vessel on the left is a lightship. The distinction is made between the north and south stations for clarity, but Wexford (North) has been known since 1966 as Wexford (O'Hanrahan).

A calm day in Wexford, as empty fertiliser wagons from Waterford make their way along the riverside towards Wexford (North) station. This was a Sunday, 24 August 1980. Few freight trains ever ran on Sundays.

A classic view of a single-cabbed B121 crossing the Crescent Bridge in Wexford on a hazy afternoon. The date is in the 1970s.

Crossley-powered 'C' class locomotive C230 is in charge of the Wexford–Waterford goods on 27 March 1963. The train will proceed to Ballygeary goods yard at Rosslare, reverse, and continue to Waterford. The locomotive wears the green livery of the late 1950s to early 1960s. *(Roger Joanes)*

J15 class 0-6-0 No 111 is pictured with the 12:45 Wexford (North) to Rosslare Harbour goods train on 11 November 1961. The train is pictured at Wexford (South) the original Waterford & Wexford Railway Co. terminus before it was linked via the Harbour tramway and Crescent Bridge to the North station. *(Norman Foster)*

Locomotive 018 pauses at Wexford (South) awaiting the signal for the way ahead on 26 May 1982. This is a laden fertiliser train from Shelton Abbey to Ennis, via Waterford and Limerick. The station remains very neat and tidy, despite being closed to public traffic. The remaining sidings appear to have recently been used for loading ballast.

In August 1998, the area formerly occupied by Wexford (South) station, here seen on the left hand side of the track, had been largely built over. Further work is in progress. Here, on 8th, empty bagged cement wagons pass en route to Limerick via Rosslare Strand with locomotive 163. For comparison with the previous photo, note the position of the signal cabin.

A similar train a little further along, in the hands of two 121 class locomotives, 129 and 134. The latter was one of the last pair of these locomotives in use, and is now preserved by the Railway Preservation Society of Ireland. The date was 4 August 1998. At the rear of the train, the land on the right was at one time home to the Smith Group engineering works into which there was a siding. This was long gone by the time these pictures were taken, but was still in place in the late 1960s.

A 29000 class railcar hurries past the site of the short-lived Felthouse Junction en route from Dublin (Connolly) to Rosslare Europort on 16 June 2016. The train had left Dublin at 13:36. In the foreground is the trackbed of the former direct curve to connect with the South Wexford line. This line opened in 1906 but was closed in 1912.

On 2 November 1996 a laden beet special is an unusual sight in Rosslare Strand with locomotive 080. At this time, all beet trains were loaded in Wellington Bridge and proceeded west to Limerick Junction and onwards to Mallow sugar factory. However in this instance the train has left Wellington Bridge in the opposite direction. The reason was that four days earlier a crane had blown down at Belview Yard in Waterford. As a result, falling debris had damaged the track and blocked the line nearby. Trains were therefore diverted by a very considerable distance, having to travel to here, run round, depart for Dublin, and proceed from there out onto the Cork main line, and back down to Mallow.

001 class locomotive 026 heads nine Mk 2 coaches south of Rosslare Strand on the final leg of its journey from Dublin (Connolly) with the 13:35 train to Rosslare Harbour on 24 August 1991. This was the last main line to have regular haulage with this class of locomotive.

No 158 is in charge of an empty bagged cement train from Wexford to Waterford at Rosslare Strand on 25 July 1998. The fine array of semaphore signals will be noted. Passengers for Dublin await their train on the down platform.

On 26 May 1982, 071 class No 080 retains its original livery, with a non-standard brownish shade of the normal colour and a non-standard CIÉ logo on the front. This was the 'delivery livery' from General Motors six years earlier, and was replaced by standard CIÉ colours the first time they were repainted. Pictured here entering Rosslare Strand en route with the 17:45 from Rosslare Harbour to Dublin, its train consists of carriages of a number of types, both steel-bodied 'Cravens' and older timber-framed types.

A spotless locomotive 048 heads two 'Park Royal' coaches and a 'BR' generating van south of Rosslare Strand on 24 August 1991. The train is the 12:45 (summer only) Waterford–Rosslare Harbour service, in this case with a very respectable load of over 100 passengers. Its return trip at 15:15 had perhaps twenty passengers.

Both the locomotive and the two carriages are 36 years old, dating from 1955. This route plus its extension to Limerick, was one of the last refuges of this type of carriage – the last timber-framed passenger stock in regular use in Ireland. It is believed that one of this pair is No 1944, now preserved on the Downpatrick & Co Down Railway.

The evening sun casts long shadows over a goods train at Rosslare Strand en route from Wexford to Waterford in September 1975. The track in the former bay platform on the left has only recently been lifted. On the right hand side, an old Great Southern Railways enamel bilingual sign indicates the 'General Waiting Room'. Ladders and a paint pot on the left show that station painting is in progress.

B145 and No 172 head a seaside excursion from Wexford to Rosslare Harbour as it enters Rosslare Strand on Sunday 3 August 1975. These trains carried considerable numbers of passengers, as can be seen with two locomotives and nine coaches. The trespass warning sign on the end of the platform on the left is by then a 70-year old relic, still headed 'Great Southern & Western Railway', and still to be seen at many stations across the former GSWR system at the time. Such cast-iron signs, and their many counterfeit equivalents, are highly sought-after collectors' items today.

Locomotive 054 approaches Rosslare Strand with the 14:55 Rosslare Harbour to Dublin (Connolly) on 24 August 1991. The line towards the harbour may be seen curving away towards the left in the background. Today, coastal erosion is a major problem in this area.

Kilrane had a high loading platform for sugar beet on the site of an original station which closed in 1970. The last passenger train to serve this station, of which by now no trace whatsoever exists, was a GAA special train on 11 October that year. Here, the early morning train at 06:40 from Waterford to Rosslare Harbour passes by on 15 August 1976, hauled by No 185.

No 074 hauls a Rosslare Harbour to Dublin train past the erstwhile Kilrane station on 7 June 2003. The remains of the former passenger platform may be seen beside the track. The beet siding has now been lifted, but the old beet platform remains on the right.

ROSSLARE HARBOUR

On 23 May 1965 the *Saint David* docked at the new arrangements at Rosslare pier and it was the start of a new era. Motor vehicles were driven off the side of the ship and across the new roadway over the viaduct. This marked the end of the 'Car Dock' and the removal of associated sidings so that the roadway could be widened. It also marked the end of the 'Motor Train' which transported passengers and their cars to/from Ballygeary. Motorists arriving had their cars lifted by crane from the ship's hold, pushed off the sling mats and then drove their vehicle onto the car train. The driver and passengers then travelled in a carriage next to the engine. The Pilot loco hauled the train towards Kilrane and reversed it into the car dock on the mainland at Ballygeary. The drivers had to – with difficulty sometimes – reverse their cars off the train. There was no guard; the shunter on duty directed the movement but there are no files at the National Archives Kew which authorised this movement.

On the quayside, in 1906, three electric cranes were provided, all of 1½ ton capacity supplied by Stothert & Pitt, Bath, using DC at 500v. There was no national supply of electricity at that time, and the F&RR&H Co. installed two 40hp Crossley gas-engines in the gas-house adjoining the loco shed for generating current. This system was used until 1936, when a connection was taken from the power-lines of the national supply, by then extended to Rosslare. The AC current supplied was converted by a mercury-arc rectifier to provide DC for the cranes. The rectifier failed on several occasions, and some days would elapse before a new one could be brought. These rectifiers cannot be held as spare, since they deteriorate in storage out of use – the method was rather obsolete. From about 1960–1964, whenever a failure occurred, one of the D Class Diesel-Electric shunting locos was sent to Rosslare and placed in the short siding beside the power-house, it's generator being connected-up to the power-line for the cranes. This system was a complete success. In 1964 a second mercury-arc rectifier was installed and used during alternate weeks to avoid deterioration. This second rectifier made by the Hewittic Co. had been formerly used on the Hill of Howth Tramway.

With heavy items of cargo increasing, the F&RR&H purchased, in 1936, a 5 ton crane from Smith & Co. In 1957 with container traffic rapidly advancing, a 7½ ton electric crane was supplied, also by Smith. All the cranes up to then had travelled on a 7' gauge track, and by laying one length of rail and utilising one of the original rails, a mixed gauge was provided, accommodating the 12' gauge of the new 7½ ton crane.

For many years the main purpose of Rosslare was the BR sailings to Fishguard and the writers can recall the *Caledonian Princess* and *Avalon* among others on these sailings. The *Saint David*, with FR on the funnel, was withdrawn in 1971. Also in 1971 BR introduced the brand name 'Sealink'. However, there were sailings to Pembroke operated by the B&I, later taken over by Irish Ferries. The B&I line introduced *Viking III* for the start of services in May 1980. It was not until Irish Ferries took over in 1992 that the vessels could compete with the Fishguard service. The arrival of the *Isle of Innisfree (II)* raised standards considerably.

In 1968 Normandy Ferries commenced sailings between Rosslare and Le Havre with one round trip per week. After a short absence in 1972, the Irish Continental Line, a subsidiary of Irish Shipping, resumed services in 1973 using the *Saint Patrick*. Services were increased to three return sailings per week. A management buyout created Irish Ferries in 1985 as a result of Irish Shipping going into liquidation. By the end of the 20th century sailings were operating every second day to either Cherbourg and Roscoff.

The story of continual expansion at Rosslare received a considerable boost because of

Brexit in 2020. Freight companies were keen to avoid the landbridge in the UK and the serious delays that had resulted from Britain leaving the EU. Reviewing the situation in early 2023 there were fifteen sailings each way between Rosslare and France/Spain. Stena Line were serving Cherbourg three times per week using the *Stena Horizon*. Brittany Ferries with their ship the *MV Salamanca* also serve, three times per week, Bilbao (Spain) and Cherbourg. This is likely to increase in the near future. DFDS, well known for their Liner Trains, operate six days per week, usually to Dunkerque. Neptune Lines just have one sailing per week and they advertise routes to Bilbao/Le Havre/Southhampton. Trade vehicles and ro-ro freight are catered for. Finally, Finnlines has two sailings per week to Zeebrugge in Belgium with the same type of freight as Neptune.

So, as can be seen, Rosslare Harbour as a shipping port has grown in importance over the years while the railway has virtually no role. Basic facilities exist that have been provided for rail travel and space has been provided for the free flow of road traffic so that it is not blocked at level crossings.

On Sunday 27 June 1959, a J15 class 0-6-0 enters Rosslare Harbour station. The locomotive retains the all-over grey livery which was first introduced by the GSWR in the mid-1910s, while the carriage carries CIÉ's light green livery, used on coaches and diesel locomotives between 1956 and 1962. On the left there was a siding for wagons loading and unloading from ships, and the cranes used for this purpose may be seen. These cranes dated from 1906, and were built by Stothert & Pitt (Bath, UK). The train is being guided in by a disc signal, which was unusual; the reason is that the normal platform was occupied by wagons carrying a special consignment of goods. (Norman Campion)

This siding at Rosslare Harbour was called the 'Car Dock'. Vehicles arriving off the mail boats were driven onto flat wagons here to be taken across onto the mainland where they were unloaded again to be reunited with their owners and driven onwards. While the vehicles travelled thus, their owners travelled in an attached carriage. The wagon seen in this picture in June 1959 is carrying timber which has been imported for the Wexford Timber Company. The locomotive from the train mentioned above may be seen on the bridge in the background on the right. (Norman Campion)

On the same day, a large consignment of bacon from Cappoquin Bacon Factory, in British Railways 'BD' containers, awaits unloading from open wagons onto the *TSS Great Western* which sailed to Fishguard. The bacon was then taken by special train to London (Paddington) Goods Depot where an 0-6-0 condensing pannier tank locomotive was attached. The train then worked over the Circle Line of London Underground and the widened lines to Farringdon where it was shunted to Smithfield Goods Depot. Smithfield is a wholesale market opening at midnight so the Cappoquin bacon would be on retail sale in London on Monday morning. *(Norman Campion)*

On 2 July 1960, J15 class No 118 operates the car shuttle from the pier, as mentioned above. The elderly brake second coach was used to ferry the drivers across to the mainland. At this stage, the locomotive was sixty-nine years old, having been built at Inchicore Works in 1891. It would last until the end of steam operations in 1963. The

locomotive is paired with a tender formerly used on an oil-burning locomotive, hence the faded remains of a large white circle towards the rear of it. The tender has been re-converted to carry coal, and its capacity enhanced by raising its sides with wooden planks. The carriage was also elderly, some fifty years old. *(Sam Carse)*

The 'car shuttle' adjacent to the bridge at Rosslare Harbour on 2 July 1960. We are looking at the other side of the locomotive and tender, the latter having neither the white circle referred to in the last caption nor the 'flying snail' logo on this side. The carriage may be seen again, along with the first of the flat wagons for cars behind it. These flat wagons were the chassis of withdrawn six-wheeled coaches. The wagons in the foreground have an 'O' prefix to their numbers, indicating that they were for use by the Locomotive Dept. for carrying coal and locomotive ash. The tank wagon on the right is carrying diesel for use by CIÉ. *(Sam Carse)*

61

A busy day on 13 August 1970 at Rosslare. B161 arrives with the 07:20 Cork–Rosslare boat train made up of at least ten vehicles. Only three years earlier, these trains had been re-routed via Limerick Junction, following the closure of their former route along the Mallow–Fermoy–Dungarvan–Waterford line. On the left, the corner of the former signal cabin may be seen – this was burned down by accident some years later. The train on the right is the 10:50 local service to Wexford headed by a Crossley-powered 'C' class locomotive, C229. It consists of two ancient timber-bodied non-corridor third class coaches dating from the 1900–1910 period with a 'tin van' passenger brake in between, followed by (out of view) a 1950s CIÉ coach and another 'tin van'. This venerable selection was used on Rosslare–Wexford local trains. The unreliable 'C' class locomotives could hardly be trusted to travel any greater distance than this before they received their new General Motors engines.

The same day, but a different view of the above local train.

B126 leaves Rosslare on the August Bank Holiday Saturday 2 August 1975. This train is a relief extra to the 15:03 from Dublin (Connolly) to Rosslare Harbour, which had loaded to ten bogie coaches, an indication of how many people still travelled by train to ferries. The ferry is the British Rail Sealink vessel *Avalon* preparing to leave for Fishguard in South Wales.

On the site of the current passenger station at Rosslare Harbour, No 187 pauses with a goods train from Waterford in the mid-1970s. This locomotive was among the first to receive the 'Supertrain' livery after it was introduced in 1972. The former locomotive shed is in the background. The buildings and area on the left have now been cleared away and replaced by parking areas for lorries awaiting loading onto ferries for Britain, France and Spain.

Locomotive 047 has just arrived from Dublin with a heavily loaded boat train in 1984. The old harbour sea wall is on the left. This actual harbour station was closed on 14 September 1989. (S J Carse)

A panoramic view over Rosslare Port on 2 August 1975. B126 turns on the turntable; as mentioned elsewhere, even after the cessation of steam services in 1963, many turntables remained at strategic locations around the CIÉ system to enable these single-cabbed locomotives to turn. Traffic queues for the ferry, while brand new cars await loading within the railway premises. The pier seen in the distance curving out towards the crane is where the harbour terminus seen in the previous photograph is situated.

A railway enthusiast tour resulted in another member of the class turning in the same place on 25 September 2004. The extent to which the harbour pier area has changed is very evident. A considerably greater area of land has now been reclaimed and modern terminal buildings constructed in the distance.

Locomotive No 015, now preserved by the Irish Traction Group, awaits departure at Rosslare Harbour with the 14:55 Rosslare Harbour to Dublin (Connolly) on 2 July 1988. The locomotive retains its CIÉ livery but the carriages behind it have the white stripes introduced when the railway came under the name of Irish Rail / Iarnród Éireann the year before.

Locomotive No 027 has just arrived on the same day with the midday train from Dublin and runs round its train in preparation for departure as the 18:00 from Rosslare to Dublin. This location of the station, which had changed positions on a number of occasions in its history, was briefly referred to as Rosslare 'Mainland' – the track to the old harbour station may be seen in the distance.

The final terminal station was served as Rosslare Europort between 14 September 1989 and 14 April 2008. (Today's station is at the inland side of the truck parking area). Here, on 30 December 2004 large crowds have long since taken to their cars, and the 13:25 to Dublin (Connolly) is but a six-coach 2700-class suburban railcar. These units were built in Spain in 1997/8 by Alsthom in Spain.

On 14 May 2005, commuter railcars are still in use on the Rosslare service, but this time it is a 29000 class CAF-built unit commencing its journey to Dublin. The ferry is the high speed service to Pembroke Dock in South Wales.

The new 'station' at Rosslare Europort, opened on Sunday 27 April 2008, is actually no more than a railway halt, albeit at the end of the line! Moreover, it is fifteen minutes' walk from the harbour building. On 20 May 2010, a 2700 class railcar has just arrived with the 15:10 from Limerick Junction.

WATERFORD TO KILLINICK AND ROSSLARE STRAND – THE SOUTH WEXFORD LINE

Here we take a journey out from Waterford to Killinick, the station before the junction at Rosslare Strand, which location has already been covered on pages 51–55. This was one of the last through routes ever opened for traffic in Ireland, being built to connect Waterford with Rosslare Harbour, thus enabling the Great Southern & Western Railway to operate through express services between Cork and Rosslare via Mallow, Fermoy and Waterford. The initial plan had been to create an express route from London (Paddington) to Killarney via Fishguard and Rosslare. The line opened in 1906 and lasted until 2010, by which time it had for many years been operated effectively as a branch line between Waterford and Rosslare, with only a very limited service. Its main feature was the Barrow Viaduct, with opening section to allow shipping to pass from the sea, up river to New Ross.

On 28 May 1999, the 'Steel' train (imported rails) is being loaded at Waterford (East) Port for onward transport to the Permanent Way Depot at Portlaoise. New rails are nowadays loaded onto wagons down river at Belview.

On the west side of Waterford station, a siding served the R & H Hall factory for many years. Here, on 28 May 1999, locomotive 080 has sixteen four-wheel wagons containing grain to go to Port Laoise, and two empty flat wagons. The line on the left hand side is the running line out to Abbey Junction, where the routes to New Ross and Rosslare Strand will diverge. This section had been double as far as just beyond Abbey Junction, but by this stage the former westbound line (centre) is disused.

The signal cabin at Abbey Junction looking towards Waterford, 13 September 2008. The level crossing gate is of standard CIÉ design of the day.

In August 1970, 'C' class locomotive C231 shunts flat wagons into the original Bell sidings for loading. This locomotive is now restored and preserved by the Irish Traction Group and is today resident at the Downpatrick & Co Down Railway. At one time, the Bell ferry company was a major customer of CIÉ, with container trains serving destinations as far afield as Belfast. On Saturdays into the 1980s, Bell traffic was so busy in Dublin that up to five special trains had to operate on Saturdays to clear container traffic from North Wall.

A view of the original Bell yard which was built at the Frank Cassin Wharf in Waterford in 1969.

The current terminal at Belview, pictured on 4 December 1993, soon after it opened. In long winter shadows, locomotive 049 pauses during shunting manoeuvres.

Another view of Belview on the same day as No 192 passes with the 13:30 laden beet train from Wellington Bridge to Waterford. With only fifteen wagons, this train will be combined with more wagons in Waterford before proceeding

to Mallow. No 192 was seen later returning to Rosslare with the 17:00 Waterford–Rosslare Harbour passenger train.

An unusual view of the Barrow Bridge, taken from the preserved Scottish paddle steamer, *Waverley* on 7 June 1986. The bridge was being repaired following an unfortunate altercation with a river-borne vessel.

An idea of the length of the Barrow Bridge viaduct may be gained from this view which shows about three quarters of it. On 12 May 1979 a railway enthusiasts' excursion passes en route to Rosslare, before heading back up the DSER main line to Dublin. The locomotive is No 186, and the excursion was chartered jointly by the Locomotive Club of Great Britain and the Irish Railway Record Society. Until the opening of the Lagan Viaduct in Belfast, the Barrow Bridge was the longest railway bridge or viaduct in Ireland.

In the final years of passenger service over the South Wexford line, two-coach railcar sets were the norm. Here, with only months before closure, on 17 July 2010, a 2800 class railcar passes over the viaduct en route to Rosslare.

The Barrow Bridge was the major feature on the South Wexford line. Here, on 13 October 1979, it has opened to let a ship pass from New Ross port out to the sea. This delayed beet train operations for the day, as it was in the middle of the beet season.

Locomotive 031 passes the erstwhile Kilmokea Halt on 16 July 1977 with the 16:30 Waterford–Rosslare Harbour train. This train was still busy into the 1970s, hence the formation of three 'laminate' coaches, one 'Park Royal' and a generator van.

On the same day, the 15:50 Limerick–Rosslare Harbour passes Dunbrody Abbey with locomotive 017 up front.

'All Ireland Sunday', 4 September 1977, saw a GAA special from Bridgetown to Dublin (Heuston) leaving Campile. On this day, Wexford's hurlers did not prevail, being beaten in Croke Park by Cork.

An unusually long train approaches Campile on 3 September 1977 with the 18:40 from Rosslare Harbour to Limerick. Examination of the train shows the leading three coaches followed by a van – but with three more 'Park Royal' carriages added at the back. These had been added at Rosslare for working to Waterford in connection with GAA specials the following day, as referred to in the previous caption. The locomotive was No 189.

The South Wexford line was a shadow of its former self by the time this picture was taken on 12 May 2005. Only a dishevelled bus shelter serves now as a station at Ballycullane. So were the trains – here, a two-car 2600 class railcar is on the 17:30 Waterford–Rosslare service. Before the line closed, 2600 class railcars were replaced by 2800 class equivalents.

On 9 February 2002, locomotives 128 and 129 were scheduled to take ten laden cement wagons from Waterford to Wexford (via Rosslare Strand). However, things were to take a turn for the unexpected! First of all, these locomotives were called upon to rescue the 07:05 Rosslare–Waterford passenger train, leaving the cement wagons in Waterford yard, after the locomotive on that train (No 167) failed before leaving. Once the 07:05 reached Waterford with 128 and 129, they coupled up to the cement wagons to head east. But the leading locomotive, 129 (the cleaner one!) itself failed at Wellington Bridge en route. Faced with only 128 being serviceable (but facing the wrong way), the pair ran round the train and headed back to Waterford with 128 leading, as seen here at Ballycullane. The cement wagons had to await the following day before they could be brought on to Wexford. It is noted that the initial cause of the problem, No 167, was eventually able to move under its own power and travel back light to Waterford. The station building, now closed up, would later be removed entirely, and only the one through track remained.

On 6 June 1998 the Irish Railway Record Society organised an excursion over the South Wexford line using Irish Rail's 'Executive Set' – the two maroon and black coaches in the middle of the train. The locomotives were Nos 135 and 133, and it is seen here pausing at Ballycullane. This is believed to be the only time that the 'Executive' train ever traversed this line.

On the evening of 14 August 1976, the 18:30 Rosslare–Limerick train appears to be well loaded. The train, headed by B143, crosses Taylorstown Viaduct with seven coaches. The first four are the regular set, followed by a luggage brake van. This train will have no heating, as the van is not a generator van – while unusual, there was no need for heating on a beautiful summer evening! The rear two coaches have been added on, as it appears that they are being worked forward for GAA traffic the following day, when Wexford and Galway met in the All-Ireland Senior Hurling semi-final in Cork. (They drew!)

On the same day the 16:00 Limerick–Rosslare Harbour was also a longer than usual train due this time to heavier summer traffic. Here it crosses Taylorstown Viaduct with an 001 class locomotive at the front.

The early morning Waterford–Rosslare Harbour local arrives in Wellington Bridge behind re-engined 'A' class locomotive A21R, in summer 1972. (D Carse)

The 12:40 Waterford–Wexford goods train passes through Wellington Bridge on 23 September 1975. The locomotive is No 182. It will be noted that the goods train has a guard's van at both ends, to avoid shunting when reversing the train at Ballygeary. On the left is the large beet loading platform, later replaced by a new facility on the far right. The photographer's famous mini car, registered as VIM 14, was to be seen in many of his railway photographs all over the country, and is central here…

B155 pauses at Wellington Bridge with the 12:10 Waterford–Rosslare Harbour train on 23 September 1975.

018

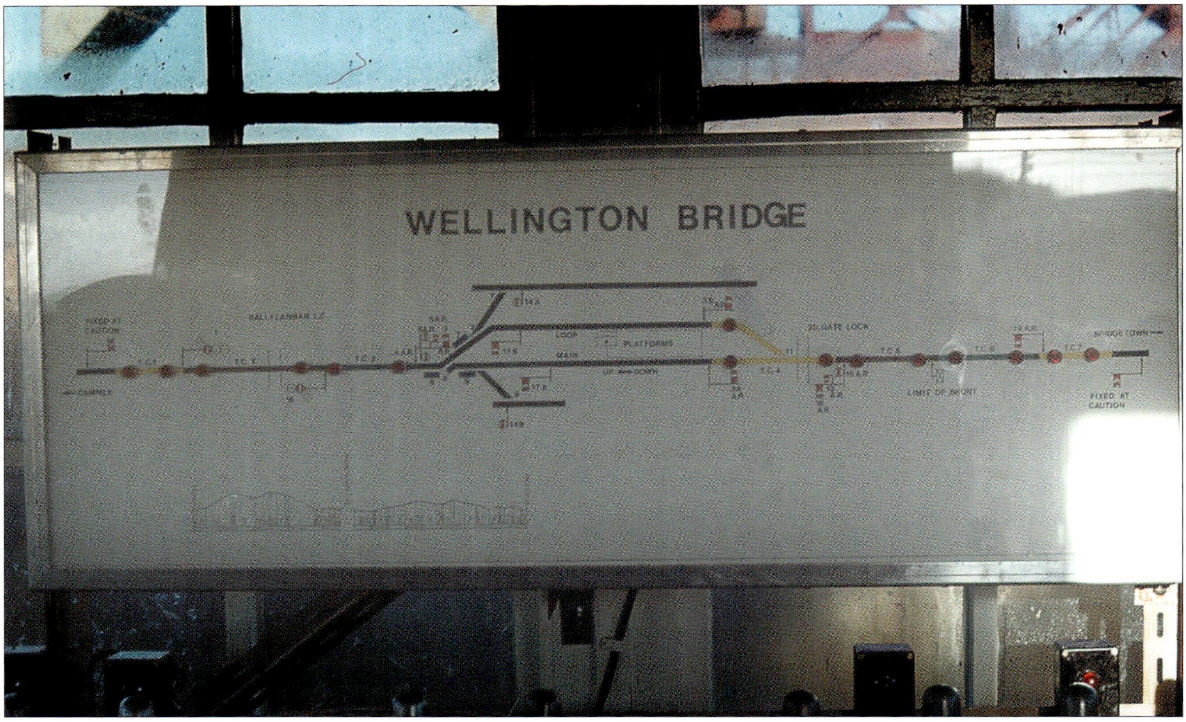
WELLINGTON BRIDGE
FIXED AT CAUTION
BALLYLANNAN L.C.
T.C.1
T.C.2
T.C.3
4.A.R.
14.A
LOOP
PLATFORMS
MAIN
UP ⟶ DOWN
17.B
17.A
14B
T.C.4
20 GATE LOCK
T.C.5
T.C.6
T.C.7
15 A.R.
19 A.R.
LIMIT OF SHUNT
BRIDGETOWN ⟶
FIXED AT CAUTION
⟵ CAMPILE

By 26 May 1982 the new beet loading facility was in operation – seen here on the far right. No 018 passes through with empty fertiliser wagons for Shelton Abbey, Co Wicklow. On arrival, 018 would collect a laden train before retracing its steps back to Waterford via Rosslare Strand, for onward transit to Ennis that day.

Signal cabin diagram, Wellington Bridge, 29 December 1979. The gradient profile of the line may be seen lower left – this shows how steeply graded the line was. The long siding shown at the top of the plan was by then the main beet loading siding, which had just opened.

On 9 February 2002, Nos 128 and 129 failed at Wellington Bridges with a laden cement train for Wexford, as explained on page 81. Here, they prepare to run round to the other end of the train in order to retreat back to Waterford.

Duncormick station closed to passengers on 6 September 1976 but is still standing here in the early 1980s. Locomotive 027 passes by with a laden fertiliser train from Shelton Abbey towards Waterford. The signal cabin was also closed by this stage.

On a Sunday, 15 March 1976, the short-lived 08:00 Rosslare Harbour–Waterford service passes through Duncormick station. While the station was still open, this train did not stop here. This service was in connection with an incoming ferry and was a rare example of Sunday passenger train on the line. The loop on the left appears not to have been regularly used in recent times.

In 2010, Duncormick was a very different sight. Here, a four coach 2800 class railcar passes by with a 'farewell' special train organised by the Irish Railway Record Society on 17 July. The line finally closed to traffic in September 2010.

On Sunday 4 September 1977, a special train left Bridgetown for Dublin (Heuston) via Waterford and Kilkenny, in connection with the All-Ireland Senior Hurling Final between Cork and Wexford. Here it is seen about to leave around 08:00 hauled by locomotives B168 and 170. (See page 79)

No 182 has the 12:40 Waterford–Wexford goods at Bridgetown on 23 September 1975. The figure on the platform the left is the well-known Dublin railway enthusiast and modeller, the late Sam Carse. The goods platform on the far left is still in use for beet traffic.

A now-forlorn looking Bridgetown in later days; by 25 July 1998, as the world panics about the 'Millenium Bug' afflicting computers, No 156 passes through with ten bagged cement wagons en route from Waterford to Wexford. These had come from Platin, Co Louth via North Wall, and down to Waterford the day before. One might wonder why they were not simply taken from Drogheda straight through to Wexford via the South-Eastern line. The answer was that there were more spare drivers for this type of traffic in Waterford at the time than in Dublin.

Approaching Killinick on 4 August 1998, locomotives 129 and 134 are in charge of a Waterford–Wexford bagged cement train.

The same train as above on its return journey with empty cement wagons. This leading locomotive is now preserved by the Railway Preservation Society of Ireland. Cables are being laid alongside the line, involving a deep trench through the former platform. Buildings and other infrastructure are long gone.

On 26 May 1982, No 018 hauls a laden Shelton Abbey–Ennis fertiliser train past Killinick. The loop has just been disconnected and is seen in the process of being lifted on the right.

CARRYING THE BEET

Our final look at the railways of the south-east focuses on what the South Wexford line became famous for in its later years – carrying sugar beet from this rich agricultural area to Thurles and Mallow sugar factories. Wellington Bridge became the last location in Ireland where this commodity would be loaded, and the sights and sounds of the heavily laden trains labouring up several steep – and scenic – gradients en route will long be remembered by those fortunate enough to witness this spectacle. Here, we retrace our steps from Kilrane, near Rosslare, back to Waterford via a series of beet trains photographed over a 32 year period, between 1974 and the end of beet traffic in 2006.

THE BEET CAMPAIGN
Barry Carse

The word campaign comes from the military precision with which the whole season was organised each year. The farmer was allotted a quota and time at the railway station to load the beet. The railway company responded with equal efficiency to transport the beet to the factories.

There were four Beet Factories. Carlow was erected by the Irish Sugar Manufacturing Co. and processing started in mid-October 1926. The other ones were at Thurles, Mallow and Tuam and their first campaigns were in 1934. By this stage Comhlucht Siuicre Eireann Teo. was established.

In 1976 beet was grown in twenty-two Irish counties with Cork having the highest number of growers. Wexford was a close second.

The Specials for the Carlow Beet Campaign 1960/61 are shown separately on pages 146–147. As regards the North Wexford, Specials numbered BC37–BC40 cover this area serving Ballywilliam, Palace East and Chapel.

Wexford supplied one empty each to Macmine, Edermine and Enniscorthy per 06:45 Goods and at the same time picked up laden beet. BC39 dealt with Killurin as can be seen for the 11:00 pm from Wexford. New Ross and Glenmore were dealt with by beet specials for Thurles. The 1962 season was the last for steam operation and J15s were used on these specials.

Beet loadings on the North Wexford were modest enough but in contrast the South Wexford was a different story with bigger quotas and many more stations. I will describe my travels on Friday 29 October 1976 when I joined the (BS 4) 04:20 empty ex-Thurles Beet Factory sidings to Ballygeary at Waterford. Driver Michael Wyse was in charge of 005 and our load was six covered wagons with pulp and 40 open wagons plus guard's van.

Also on board was Traffic Inspector Croke and he had a busy job. At each station he would note the number of wagons and would regularly send messages back to Waterford on the state of play. The guard was from Rosslare and had worked the 07:10 passenger train. We left Waterford at 08:55, five minutes early and at Campile left 15 wagons. Departure from Campile was 09:30 and we were blocked in Ballcullane by BS 1 shunting at Wellington Bridge. This had gone out around 05:00 from Waterford. We passed through Wellington Bridge at 10:00 crossing BS 1 – No 031 and about 30 wagons. At Duncormick we dropped a lot of empties but I am not sure about Bridgetown or Killinick. However at Ballygeary we still had five empty and two pulp for the return journey. Kilrane is best served on the return journey given the layout of the points so this is why we went into Ballygeary to run around and departure at 11:56. At Kilrane there was six off and seven on, Killinick six on, Bridgetown 14 on, Duncormick eight on, so that by Wellington Bridge we left a few laden wagons behind and our load was 30 for the next section to Campile. Before leaving, B169 and Guard's Van was crossed. At Campile we crossed 021 and Guard's Van. We added 13 laden beet and left with 43 wagons + Guard's Van at 15:50 reaching Waterford at 16:12. The second Rosslare Guard returned working the 16:25 passenger and I returned passenger to Dublin Heuston. Later that day there would be two more beet specials from the South Wexford to Thurles.

The Beet campaign of 2005/6 was the last and so both the authors paid a visit on Saturday 22 October 2005. By this stage Wellington Bridge was the central loading point for beet and all trains ran to Mallow Beet Factory Sidings. On arrival in Wellington Bridge at 09:10 there 89 four wheelers and 13 Bogies. Over the course of the day there were six departures as follows:

Schedule	Train	Location	Time
09:10	079 + 13 bogies	Wellington Bridge	dep. 09:35
10:45	082 + 25 wagons	Wellington Bridge	dep. 11:02
12:25	134/176 + 25 wagons	Ballycullane	pass 12:48
14:00	124/147 + 25 wagons	Campile	pass 14:27
15:35	072 + 25 wagons	Ballycullane	pass 15:45
18:09	124/147 + 25 wagons	Taylorstown	pass 16:25

There were two empty trains and these brought out 45 between them bringing the total to 134.

If you subtract the five trains of 25 wagons each you are left with nine laden at 16:45, which we checked out. Certainly a busy day and well worth the trip to South Wexford.

The Beet Campaign finished on 31 March 2006. Changes to the common agricultural policy shifted sugar production from Europe to developing countries. There were no more Beet Campaigns for the railway. Greencore, the former Irish Sugar Company, closed it's factories at Carlow and Mallow.

Kilrane was a loading place for sugar beet until 7 March 1977. Here, locomotive 026 has a 'PalVan' to carry beet pulp, and six empty beet wagons on 6 November 1976, during the last beet season in which beet was loaded here. To the left of the train at the loading bank are another six laden beet wagons, with another load dumped to the left awaiting loading. A tractor and trailer arrives on the far left with another load, while four goods vans are to be seen in the distance, having brought in beet pulp for the local farmers. The photographer recalls this being a very cold day!

Locomotive 005 shunts at Kilrane on 29 October 1976; laden beet wagons and vans for beet pulp are evident. Beet trains were still loose-coupled at this time, hence the presence of a guard's van. The train is the return working of the 09:00 empty beet special from Waterford to Ballygeary. A ground frame controlled access to these sidings.

The original Ballygeary Kilrane station platform and building was exactly where locomotive 158 is seen in this picture, but was cleared away in 1970 to be replaced by the high beet loading bank beside the locomotive. Beet loading banks were designed to be considerably higher than normal platforms to enable trailers and trucks to tip beet directly into open wagons. A tractor and trailer are seen in the distance. To the right, the goods vans are an interesting collection. The one closest to the camera is an ex-Great Northern Railway cement van of 1954 vintage. Beyond it is a CIE 'PalVan' of 1965 origin, and a standard CIE 'H' van beyond that. A laden beet wagon is seen to the left with the detached guard's van in the distance. This duty was carried out by the Wexford pilot locomotive which by this stage had little else to do all day. The date is 22 January 1977, late in the beet season which normally finished by around New Year's Day.

On 6 November 1976, No 026 heads twelve empty beet wagons and two vans containing beet pulp on the approach to Killinick.

On the same day as the above, No 026 returned later in the day towards Waterford. At Killinick the winter sun illuminates the train as it passes through with the 13:10 laden departure from Ballygeary. The line in the centre is the passenger loop which served the other side of the main platform, while the right-hand track is the goods loop, still then in use for beet. While this train did not stop here, it proceeded to add another 14 wagons at Bridgetown and a further nine at Duncormick, making a total of 30 wagons and

a guard's van leaving Duncormick for Campile. Leaving Campile, further wagons could be added up to a total of 43, for the run into Waterford and on to Thurles Sugar Factory.

Locomotive 040 shunts in Killinick approximately 1974. On the right, a long line of beet wagons is actually in two sections. The laden wagons await adding to this train, while the empty ones at the back have been dropped off by an eastbound train for loading. Behind the locomotive is a single wagon of beet, collected at Kilrane, and several empty vans returning to Thurles Sugar Factory after bringing beet pulp to local stations.

On a very wet 4 November 1978, No 059 heads through Bridgetown towards Killinick with the 09:00 empty beet wagons from Waterford. Laden wagons await collection in the other direction on the left, with pulp vans in the distance. This train had left Waterford with 38 wagons, and dropped off 14 at Ballycullane and six at Duncormick. The remainder were for Killinick. The photographer recalls that for much of the day the skies were almost too dark to obtain a decent photograph, or it was raining…

Shunting is in progress with No 158 on 22 January 1977 at Bridgetown. The semaphore signals are of older pre-CIÉ design. The shunting signal controlling this movement may be seen adjacent to the right-hand parapet of the bridge in the distance.

The sun is out at Bridgetown on a winter day in 1974 as No 040 arrives with a westbound laden beet train which had originated in Ballygeary. Behind the locomotive is a standard goods van, followed by the laden beet wagons. Unusually, beyond this, is a CIE container on a flat wagon, followed by more vans. This container has been pressed into service due to a shortage of goods vans to carry beet pulp; it is the only instance of such a use being made of a container that the authors are aware of.

The same train as seen previously – what appears on examination to be quite a complex shunting operation is in progress; one assumes that the ultimate aim is to have all the laden beet wagons on the train, with all the empty goods vans (plus the container) together, before proceeding towards Waterford.

On 6 November 1976, the 09:00 beet empties leave Duncormick for Bridgetown in the care of locomotive 026. This was the last of the former 'A' class locomotives to be re-engined.

At Duncormick, 026 is again in evidence on the same day with its train of empty wagons and laden pulp vans. Farmers have assembled on the former goods platform on the left with trailer loads of beet.

In autumn 1974, Duncormick was still signalled and the cabin (previously seen on page 88) was still open. No 040 passes through with a laden beet train for Thurles.

Just outside Wellington Bridge, the 15:00 Waterford–Killinick empty wagons pass over the Corock River Bridge on 16 October 1976, with locomotive 050.

No 011 arrives at Wellington Bridge with 12 laden wagons on 19 November 1977. The 13 laden wagons on the right would be added here before the train continued to Waterford. A further five were added at Ballycullane and seven at Campile.

DROICHEAD EOIN
WELLINGTON BRIDGE

A busy scene on a dull day at Wellington Bridge on the same date. In typical 'beet season' weather, much is to be seen here. Farmers unload beet on the bank on the left, while around 20 wagons await loading there. On the right at the platform is the laden train with locomotive 011. On the far right more laden beet wagons can be seen; in total, there were some 45–50 wagons in this location at this time on that date.

The new loading system at Wellington Bridge was commissioned in October 1979. In December of that year, a general view shows loading in progress, still with loose-coupled wagons. The letter 'B' crudely painted on the wagons indicated that they were reserved for beet traffic. On some, the dates '77', '78' and '79' may be seen adjacent

to the 'B'; these indicated that in those years, inspections of the wagon concerned had resulted in it being passed for use that year. At least one wagon (on the right) is overloaded – this explains why Waterford and other stations along the 'beet route' had healthy populations of well fed rats during beet season, feasting on a linear row of fallen beets along the railway!

As referred to above, fallen beet is seen scattered all over the track at Wellington Bridge on 3 November 1984. 001 class locomotives dominated beet traffic at this time and here 033 and 052 have laden specials about to leave. No 033 is leaving here at 12:28, with 052 following at 13:30.

A good view of the new beet loading facility on 3 November 1984, by which time all beet loading was concentrated at Wellington Bridge. Wagons were moved up and down the loading siding by the electrically powered 'beetle', seen to the right of the wagon about to be loaded. A massive stockpile of beet awaits behind the wagons – this was put into wagons by tractor-based loaders on the ground.

071 class No 080 arrives with empty wagons on 14 December 2001 at Wellington Bridge, while a pair of 14_ class locomotives await westbound departure for Mallow in the distance. By now, the wagon storage siding on the left is placed where the old beet loading bank used to be, before the modern facility on the far right was opened.

Nos 134 and 176 await loading on 22 October 2005, the last winter of beet traffic by rail. They would work the 12:25 laden train from Wellington Bridge to Mallow Beet Factory. The spilt beet by the lineside is largely a thing of the past now, with high-sided 'double-decker' wagons.

On 22 October 2005 locomotives 134 and 176 are seen during shunting at Wellington Bridge. (*Jonathan Beaumont*)

A good view may be had here of a standard 'double-decker' wagon (right) and the unique No 27504 (left). The latter was a one-off which appeared in traffic only in the final 2005/6 season. It was painted dark blue, but with the normal brown chassis. This is where the old loading bank had been.

Another type of rolling stock which only saw use in the last beet season were the container-based bogie wagons, seen in the foreground. Northern Ireland Railways No 112 has arrived behind them with a train of empty 'double-deckers'. This locomotive was on loan to Iarnród Éireann at

the time and featured to a great extent in this last winter of beet traffic, amongst other operations. No 112 will detach from its train here and push the bogie 'container' wagons forwards across the level crossing out of the picture to the right. Once the laden train seen in the distance departs (hauled by a pair of 141 class locomotives), it will haul the containers into the line on the far side of the station building, before coupling up to the far end of the 'double-deckers' to shunt them to the loading bank later on. Another train of laden wagons awaits departure on the left. With two passenger trains per day still serving this route, the South Wexford line could be extremely busy even as late as 2005 during the beet season. Sadly, it would not last much longer. This picture was taken on 18 November 2005.

The shunting operation, described previously, in progress, No 112 re-enters Wellington Bridge with the bogie wagons as mentioned above.

On 12 October 1991, No 049 crosses Taylorstown Viaduct with empty 'double-deckers' for Wellington Bridge.

Just west of Wellington Bridge, locomotive 014 skirts the picturesque Owenduff River on 29 December 1979 with 60 empty wagons (and a guard's van) to go to Wellington Bridge for loading.

Locomotive 050 is seen here in the cutting at Taylorstown Bank – the sound of a locomotive labouring up this incline with a heavy load was not to be forgotten! Due to the steep ruling gradient, loads were restricted on this section to 30 wagons laden. The train is the 12:15 from Wellington Bridge to Waterford on 13 October 1979, fully loaded to 30 wagons plus guard's van.

In the same location on 16 November 1985, locomotive 020 has 18 'double-decker' wagons – this being the maximum permitted load of this type over this section. However, this class of locomotive was passed to haul up to 28 of this type of wagon, laden, between Campile, Waterford and Thurles.

A pleasant evening shot at Ballycullane in 1974. No 040 arrives with a laden beet train. The signalman exchanges staffs with the driver. This station was closed as a block post in 1980. (D Carse)

The height of the beet loading banks, often raised from older goods platforms, is evident here on 16 October 1976, as B153 shunts wagons. This locomotive was on duty as the Wexford pilot locomotive at the time, and, as mentioned before, could be called upon to handle beet traffic between local stations in the area. The local farmers have brought several loads in trailers.

Stations on the South Wexford line all had a fairly standard layout with a central island platform and a goods loop or siding on one side. Ballycullane was no different. Here, on 7 January 1978, No 034 waits in order to cross a train coming the other way. This locomotive had left Waterford that morning with 60 empty wagons, ending up at Killinick after dropping wagons off at various locations en route. At that point, the locomotive collected these laden wagons for return.

On the same day as the above, the eastbound train now pulls in with 059 up front. In this case it consists just of an engine and van, travelling towards Killinick in order to bring back more laden wagons.

Locomotive No 033 passes through Ballycullane with empty wagons on 16 November 1985. By now, the sidings in the foreground have been lifted, though the station building, now boarded up, remains. The train is the 09:30 from Thurles to Wellington Bridge.

On the same day, the winter sun illuminates 033 very nicely as it passes Ballycullane in the other direction with the 14:45 laden from Wellington Bridge to Campile, where it left its load of 14 wagons. The locomotive then returned light to Wellington Bridge to collect a further 14 wagons, which were then combined at Campile to make up the maximum load of 28 to go to Thurles.

121 class locomotives either in pairs themselves, or paired with members of the 141/181 class, were regulars in later years after the 001 class were withdrawn in the 1990s. Here, on 3 November 1990, 122 and the now-preserved 134 pass by Ballycullane with 18 laden 'double-deckers'. The absence of the passing loop and goods sidings on the right is evident.

In the same location as the photo of 034 and 059 on 7 January 1978 on page 117, Nos 147 and 124 pass with the 11:40 empty train from Waterford to Wellington Bridge, with just nine wagons on 22 October 2005.

Looking the other way from the photograph above, Nos 166 and 169 pass Ballycullane at 11:53 with a laden train at the very end of the sugar beet era; 27 January 2006. While beet traffic normally ended around the time of New Year, in this last season it had something of an Indian summer. The last operations ever, were as late as 31 March. The 'container' wagons are in evidence for their first and last season.

An empty train is pictured at Burkestown level crossing (near Ballycullane) on 29 November 1980, hauled by No 164.

A very lengthy empty train, loaded to sixty wagons plus a guard's van, heads away from Campile towards Ballycullane on 30 December 1982, headed by Nos. 147 and 162.

On the same day at the same place, No 006 passes in the other direction with a laden train of 30 wagons (ultimately) for Thurles. As seen previously, the practice was for the locomotive to leave these wagons at Campile and go back to Wellington Bridge for another 30 wagons. With 60 now in Campile, 006 would go forward with the maximum load of 43. Meanwhile, another locomotive would come out from Waterford to clear the remaining 17, perhaps with a further trainload having arrived there in the meantime to be added onto that!

Campile station was in an attractive setting with a rock cutting at one end. On 16 October 1976, the Wexford pilot locomotive, B153, has arrived with a laden train which may be seen out in the cutting. The locomotive has detached in order to run forward (to the left) and propel more laden wagons out of the goods loop in the foreground, which will be added to the front of the train. Meanwhile, locomotive 050 (on the right), being a more powerful locomotive, will take the combined laden train on to Waterford, while B153 will return light to Wexford.

This view on 29 October 1976 shows the sheer complexity of the beet traffic operations on the South Wexford line. No 005 has an empty goods van for beet pulp and a long train of laden wagons on the left, while the rest of the station is choked with more laden wagons; there are some 60 laden wagons here at least. The train is headed for Waterford (far end of the photograph) and has run round to this end via the loop on the far right.

No 033 arrives at Campile on 14 October 1978 with a laden train from Killinick at 14:42. As usual, four goods vans to carry beet pulp are included – overall, there are 28 laden beet wagons including the one at the front. The cabin is still open. The train added more wagons here, up to the maximum of 43 – but also a guard's van and the four empty vans – over its official limit!

On the same day, the far end of Campile station is busy, with a row of goods vans on the left, probably in connection with pulp traffic, a laden train on the main line in the middle, and 059 passing by with 19 empty wagons on the right. This working is the 15:05 from Waterford to Killinick. The siding just visible on the extreme right is the former 'Co-Op' siding, to serve the local Shelbourne Co-Operative Society. The premises of this body were subjected to the attention of German bombers during the Second World War…

On 30 December 1982, locomotives 147 and 162 arrive at Campile with a full complement of 60 empty wagons and guard's van en route to Wellington Bridge.

On 3 November 1990, a pair of 121 class locomotives (134 and 122) pass the historic Dunbrody Abbey en route to Wellington Bridge to bring a load of laden wagons back to Waterford. These two locomotives spent the day going back and forward to collect more laden wagons.

A classic view of a loose-coupled sugar beet train as it crosses the Campile River near Dunbrody Abbey in bright winter sunshine on 29 November 1980. The locomotive is No 164 heavily loaded with 34 wagons and a van and the train left Campile at 14:23. The sunny weather belies the fact that it was a very cold day.

On the Kilmokea side of Dunbrody Abbey (visible in the background), a pair of 141 class locomotives (144 and 176) lead 25 'double-deckers' towards Waterford with the 10:45 departure from Wellington Bridge. This was the last beet season and the farmers were determined to get the most out of it. This picture was taken on the unusually early date of 24 September 2005, but while this season started early, it also went on very late, with final trains running on 31 January 2006, a good four and a half months later. Normal beet 'campaigns' lasted around three months. The final train that year was the 621st one of that season.

With a full load, locomotive 009 labours past the high road bridge at Kilmokea at 11:38 on 22 November 1980. The train would have left Wellington Bridge about 11:00.

The tide is low under the Barrow Viaduct on 29 November 2004, as locomotives 149 and 160 cross with a laden train which had left Wellington Bridge at 13:00.

At the same spot fourteen years earlier, on 3 November 1990, the now-preserved No 134 and sister locomotive 122 cross the Barrow Bridge Viaduct with a train of 35 empty wagons for Wellington Bridge.

Just west of Belview, 071 class No 078 passes with a train of empties on 21 October 1995. This train left Mallow for Wellington Bridge at 08:00 with 30 'double-deckers'.

On 6 October 1984 shortly before the close of the loose-coupled era, No 038 hurries a full complement of wagons near Belview en route to Thurles. These trains travelled via Limerick Junction rather than via Kilkenny due to the necessity to reverse twice on the latter route. The train arrived at Abbey Junction at 14:25, before leaving Waterford at 15:05. At Carrick-on-Suir, the train crossed an empty beet train coming the other way, a train of ballast hoppers at Clonmel, and the 15:55 Limerick–Rosslare Harbour passenger train at Cahir.

View from the cab of the 11:40 laden train from Ballygeary to Thurles on 29 October 1976 near Snow Hill tunnel at the Barrow Bridge. The locomotive was No 005.

Class leader No 071 passes Belview container yard on 7 December 1996. The train was of 36 empty 'double-deckers'.

On a bright and sunny 4 December 1993, locomotive 190 passes east of Belview yard with the 11:50 laden train of 15 'double-deckers'.

Here we see a train of 25 laden wagons heading in the other direction hauled by 071 class No 072 on 21 October 1995.

On 6 October 1984, No 001 passes near Belview with over 50 empty wagons for Wellington Bridge.

Locomotives 170 and 169 head a laden train into Waterford past Abbey Junction on 20 November 1998. The train was running early. This picture was taken at 10:00 which happened to be the exact time that the train was scheduled to have left Wellington Bridge! Therefore, it must have left some 40 minutes early. The signal cabin can be seen in the distance. The track to the right of the train was the then-disused second track out to the junction, and the derelict siding seen on the bottom right led into the former Hall's Mills.

Swansong of beet; in the last season locomotives 160 and 144 take an empty train of the then-new container wagons out towards Abbey Junction en route to Wellington Bridge. These wagons were only in traffic a short time before beet traffic was withdrawn for ever. The train left Waterford at 11:40. The same three tracks as seen on the previous page are visible here, but looking in the other direction. On the left, the Hall's Mill siding has not been used for some time, although it would later come back into use. The former second track out to Abbey Junction (behind the photographer) is seen in the middle. All trains were then using the right-hand track.

Many of Ireland's railways were built with agricultural traffic in mind from the outset. The sudden end of the carriage of sugar beet by rail heralded the end of the relationship between Ireland's agricultural community and the railway. On Tuesday 31 January 2006, the 621st beet train of the 2005/6 season left Wellington Bridge at 18:30, and Waterford at 22:15 for Mallow. It was hauled by locomotive No 081, and consisted of 16 laden 'double-deckers'. History had been made, though the occasion went by largely unremarked. In Mallow, Ireland's last sugar factory closed for good on 15 March 2006, the end of an era and some eighty years since the first beet trains in 1926.

SEQUEL

At the time of writing, while public passenger services over the South Wexford line finished in September 2010, the line remains technically open. However, there have been no regular services of any type since that date. Some one-off train movements have taken place, the most common being in connection with inspections of the line by railway staff, and the twice-yearly weed spraying train. The track has been maintained on the basis of being passable.

The Sperry train (an inspection train) hauled by 077 passes through Campile on 6 May 2017. It was scheduled to leave Waterford at 09:00, travel to Rosslare Europort, and then return again to Waterford at 14:10. *(Tommy Johnson)*

On 26 February 2019, Inspection Car No 721 (unofficially named 'Jess') passes over Taylorstown Viaduct while working a 14:00 Rosslare Strand to Waterford routine inspection operation. It had left Greystones that morning at 10:46, first operating to Rosslare Europort and continuing later to Waterford. *(Tommy Johnson)*

On the last day of May 2021 an MPV (Multi Purpose Vehicle) worked from Wexford to Rosslare Strand at 09:00, leaving there at 09:40 for Waterford. Later in the afternoon it returned along the same route. Numbered 790, this vehicle is variously used for weedspray services and also for spraying 'Sandite', a material used to coat rail surfaces to improve locomotive adhesion during the autumn leaf fall season. In order to perform this task, it sprays the rail surfaces first with high pressure water jets. On this occasion weed spraying was the task in hand. No 790

has sprayed the South Wexford line since 2019 after the locomotive-hauled spray train ceased operations in 2018. It is seen here approaching overbridge OBH200 between Bridgetown and Duncormick. *(Tommy Johnson)*

Of the routes covered in this book, only the Rosslare Europort to Wexford line remains open, with trains continuing to Dublin. Trains no longer serve Rosslare Harbour terminal building, having been cut back to a quite dismal halt-like terminus about ten minutes' walk away in April 2008. Services are now passenger only. Here we see an 'ICR' (Inter City Railcar) passing the site of Felthouse Junction with the 13:33 Dublin (Connolly) to Rosslare Harbour Europort train on 30 June 2021. The former spur line to Killinick veered away through the bushes on the right.

LOCOMOTIVES AND PASSENGER CARRIAGES USED ON THE LINES COVERED

The locomotives seen in the foregoing pictures are of the various standard classes used on the CIÉ/IE system during the periods covered. Initially classed by letter, after 1972 these prefixes were dropped as locomotives were repainted from the predominately black livery variations into the new orange and black 'Supertrain' livery (named after a then-current advertising campaign for main line rail travel).

The letter prefixes had dated from a time when it was necessary to distinguish a diesel locomotive number from a steam equivalent; thus a locomotive numbered '17' in the 1950s would have been a steam engine, while A17 was a diesel.

LOCOMOTIVES

A/001 Class: A1–A60, later A1R–A60R, later 001–060

Introduced in 1955 with Crossley engines, these were unsatisfactory initially until the Crossley units were replaced between 1969 and 1971 by General Motors engines. In this guise, these locomotives were given a new life and took over many main line passenger services. The last examples remained in traffic until 1995. Several are preserved by the Irish Traction Group, one in working order at the Downpatrick & Co Down Railway. Another is a centrepiece in 'Hell's Kitchen' (Castlerea) Railway Museum in Co Roscommon.

C/201 Class: C201–C234, later B201–B234, later 201–234

These were smaller versions of the 'A' class above, delivered between 1956 and 1958 for branch lines. Unfortunately, not only did they suffer the same unreliability with the Crossley engines, most of the branch lines for which they were designed closed a few years later anyway, and they spent most of the 1960s on shunting and short trip duties. Like the 'A' class, they received new engines between 1969 and 1972; two with Maybach engines and the rest with General Motors units. They graduated towards Dublin suburban services in the 1970s, and after these services were electrified in the 1980s they were all withdrawn, the last in 1986. Two have been preserved by the Irish Traction Group.

B101/101 Class: B101–B112, later 101–112

Introduced in 1956, these locomotives were also known as the 'Sulzers' due to their engines, and spent most of their time working out of Cork and Waterford. They were very much considered as 'Southern' engines, as they were to be seen primarily on the Kerry–Cork and Limerick lines, Limerick–Waterford, and Cork–Mallow–Waterford–Rosslare lines. By the time the B141 and B181 classes arrived in the 1960s they graduated more towards goods and maintenance train use. The last example was withdrawn in 1978 and is stored by the Irish Traction Group.

B121/121 class: B121–B132, later 121–132

The arrival of these locomotives in 1961 heralded the future of Irish diesel locomotive development, being the first from the American manufacturer, General Motors. Every single diesel locomotive purchased since, of several types, has been from the same manufacturer. If their Crossley predecessors were unreliable, these 'Yanks' (as they were initially known) were the opposite. They proved their worth straight away and had a long and reliable life, the last examples remaining in traffic until 2008 by which time the last two were almost fifty years old. Unlike other main line diesels they only had a cab at one end. Initially, with turntables aplenty, they were turned at the end of a journey but latterly they ran in pairs, cabs outermost, when such facilities became few and far between. Two have been preserved by the Railway Preservation Society of Ireland and the Irish Traction Group.

B141/141 Class: B121–B177, later 121–177
B181/181 Class: B181–B192, later 181–192

The above two classes were double-cabbed developments of the B121 class, often joining them in 'pairs' especially from the 1970s onwards. The B141 class were delivered from late 1962 into 1963. The last example ended its operational career in 2011. Their outwardly similar, but slightly more powerful B181 class sisters were delivered a few years later in late 1966, with the last example withdrawn in 2009. Several examples, covering both classes, have been preserved by the Railway Preservation Society of Ireland and the Irish Traction Group.

071 Class: 071–088

In 1976, CIÉ took delivery of 18 of these locomotives, a larger and more modern successor to the 141/181 types. They were instantly employed on all types of main line passenger train, later being increasingly used for goods trains.

After the advent of large numbers of diesel railcars on passenger trains in the early 2000s they were relegated to goods and maintenance trains. From then on, passenger train workings were confined to occasional special trains for railway enthusiast groups or tourist operations.

J15/101 Class steam locomotives

These were the most numerous type of Irish steam locomotive by a very long way indeed, with 111 of them being built (with variations) between 1867 and 1903. They were the 'jack of all trades' of the Irish railway system throughout the first half of the 20th century. By the time steam traction ended on the CIÉ system in 1963, despite larger and more modern types having already been withdrawn and scrapped, more than a few of these 'old faithfuls' were still in use albeit in an appalling external state. They will have been seen in former days on all of the lines covered in this book – and much further afield too. Two are preserved by the Railway Preservation Society of Ireland.

PASSENGER CARRIAGES

'Laminate' type

This is a generic term originally used to describe coaches built at Inchicore Works during the carriage modernisation programme from 1956 to 1962. The term related to the fact that the framework was composed of laminated wood, rather than (as previously) solid timber. Latterly, the term was widely, but incorrectly, used to describe most types of coaches built not just in this period, but from the early 1950s onwards too. There were many variations. The last of these vehicles were withdrawn in 1987/8.

'Park Royal' type

Large numbers of these vehicles were introduced in 1955/56/57 to replace older coaches of various types. Some were intended initially for main line use, others for Dublin suburban traffic. They ended up being used all over the country in conjunction with other types, and the last three examples were withdrawn from the Limerick–Waterford route in 1994.

'Cravens' type

These were the first carriages ever to run in Ireland which were all-steel. The first examples were delivered as sets of parts from the firm of Cravens Ltd, of Sheffield in England, hence the name given to this design. Later examples were built in Inchicore Works. Introduced in 1963, they were initially used on main line services, but also on secondary lines from 1972 onwards, after the Mk2 stock entered traffic. However, the last examples were still in use in the opening years of the 21st century on the Limerick–Ballybrophy and Limerick–Waterford–Rosslare routes, plus the Ballina branch in Co Mayo. A number have been preserved by the Railway Preservation Society of Ireland, and have been used not only for steam and diesel-hauled RPSI excursions, but also for the Railtours Ireland 'Emerald Isle Express', which ran on a number of occasions in the late 2010s.

Mk 2

These were Ireland's first air-conditioned passenger vehicles, and were first introduced in 1972. They carried a new variation of the primarily orange-brown and black livery, with the former rather than the latter prominent. By degrees all locomotives except shunters were painted to match. They were heavily marketed under the banner of 'Supertrain', with improved speeds on some lines coming into force at the same time. They closely resembled many British coaches of the era, as the body shells were built by British Rail Engineering Ltd (BREL) rather than by CIÉ at Inchicore Works. They were the mainstay of main line passenger services until the mid-1980s, after which Mk 3 stock started to take over. The final working of Mk 2 stock was the 05:05 Athlone–Dublin commuter service on 31 March 2008.

Mk 3

Following the success of the Mk 2 stock, in 1984 a newer generation of coaches were introduced for main line use. These were the later development of the same concept as the Mk 2. Again, similarities were to be seen with some British stock due to BREL design. These carriages would give over twenty years' service, but due to a policy change in motive power, and an increasing move towards railcar trains, the last were withdrawn from normal service in 2009. Most were scrapped but a number were placed in store, as a result of which a private tourist operator paid to have a set refurbished for the Belmond Grand Hibernian tourist train which commenced seasonal operation 2016.

'BR' Generating Vans

Throughout the 1960s, all locomotive-hauled passenger trains had to carry a generating van with them to provide steam heating to carriages. Unlike in many other countries, first-generation diesel locomotives (as featured in this book) did not have the facilities to provide power to their trains. These original vans were built in several forms, some with generators and some to carry mailbags or parcels; some both. Some were built as postal sorting vans. All of these vehicles were four or six-wheeled. Due to clocking up large mileages most were worn out by the late 1960s, and replacements were needed. In addition, higher train speeds required bogie vehicles rather than these. CIÉ looked to British Rail and purchased twenty-one second-hand full brake bogie vehicles of several types. These were originally built between 1952 and 1958 by British Railways, but converted for CIÉ in 1972 by adding generating equipment and ventilators. Remaining space was used for a guard's compartment and luggage/parcels space. They were then shipped to Ireland and would operate as 'genny vans' until the last 'Craven' carriages were withdrawn.

TRACK PLANS

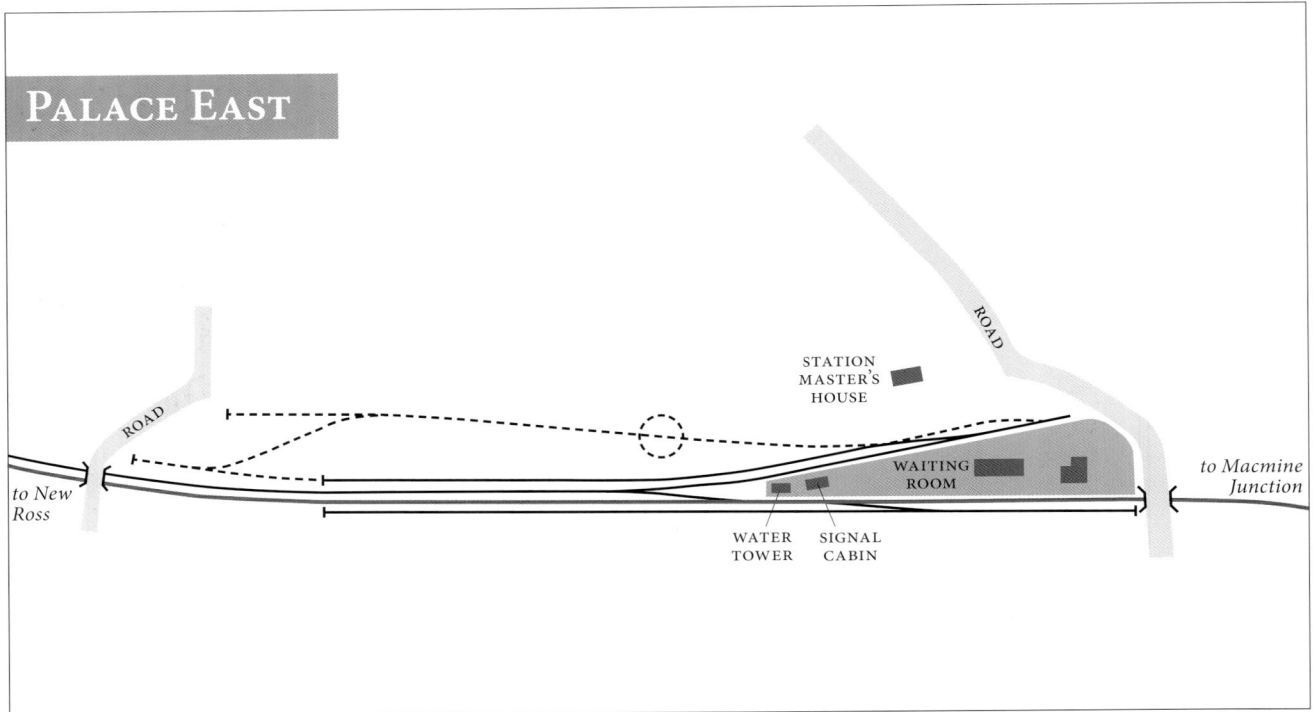

This plan is based on an early GS&WR station diagram and was probably a work in progress. The purple line likely indicates the DSER, whilst the black represents the GS&WR. The dashed lines were just at the planning stage.

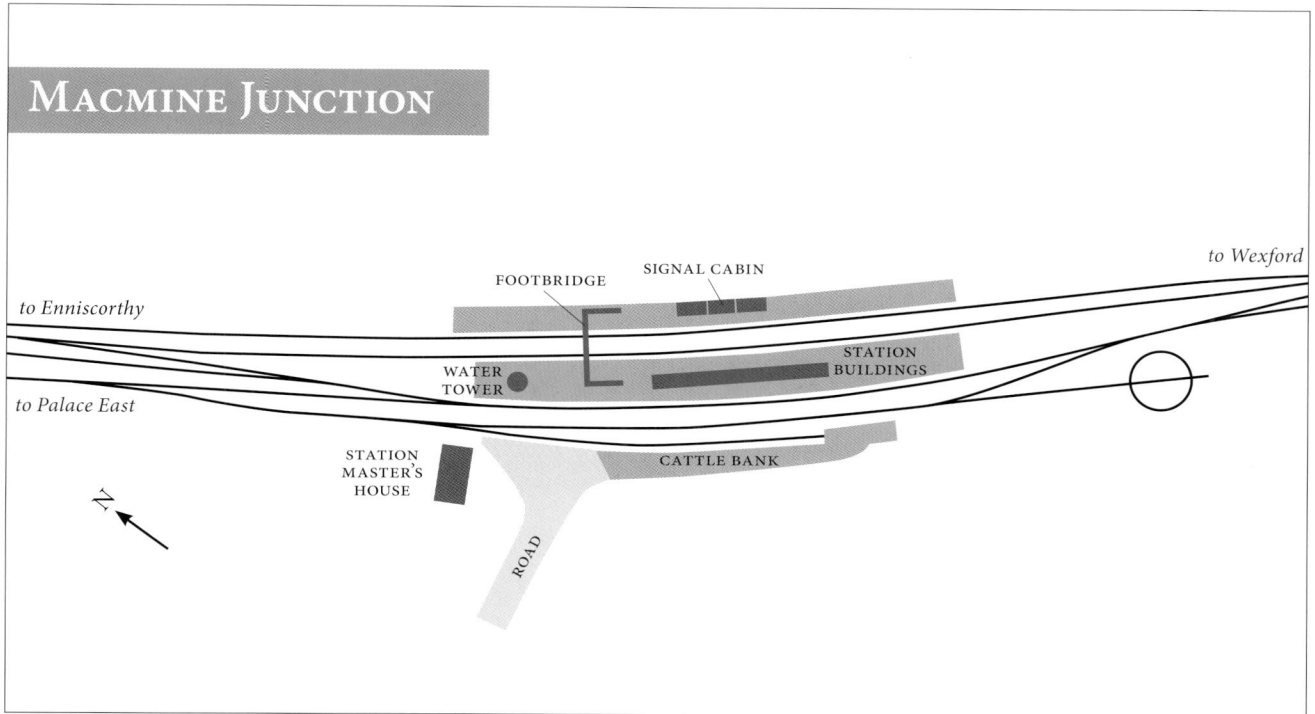

TIMETABLES

Carlow Beet Campaign 1960/61

B.C. 37.

PALACE EAST TO CARLOW
(Laden).

Commencing 14th October, 1960.

		Arr. p.m.	Dep. p.m.
Palace East	(5)	—	6 30
Ballywilliam	(7)	6 42	7 00
Ballyling	(2)	—	—
Borris	(7)	8 00	8 20
Muine Bheag		8 46	9 00
Carlow B.S.		9 30	—

Borris attach 7 laden wagons ex Goresbridge.

B.C. 38.

CARLOW TO PALACE EAST
(Empty).

Commencing 13th October, 1960.

		Arr. p.m.	Dep. p.m.
Carlow B.S.		—	2 30
Muine Bheag		3 05	3 10
Goresbridge	(7L7E)	3 28	3 45
Borris	(7)	4 00	4 15
Ballyling	(2)	—	—
Ballywilliam		pass	5 15
Palace East	(5)	5 30	—

Detach 7 laden wagons ex Goresbridge at Borris for B.C. 37.

B.C. 39.

WEXFORD TO CARLOW
(Laden).

Commencing 24th October, 1960.

		Arr. p.m.	Dep. p.m.
Wexford	(4)	—	11 00
Killurin	(2E 2L)	11 22	11 40
Macmine		pass	11 50
		a.m.	a.m.
Chapel	(4)	12 18	12 35
Palace East		1 00	1 10
Borris	(3)	1 57	2 20
Muine Bheag		2 46	3 18
Milford		pass (a)	3 32
Carlow		pass (b)	3 43
Carlow B.S.		3 55	—

(a) Cross B.C. 40.

(b) Cross 12.35 a.m. Goods.

B.C. 40.

CARLOW TO WEXFORD
(Empty).

Commencing 24th October, 1960.

		Arr. a.m.	Dep. a.m.
Carlow B.S.		—	3 10
Carlow		pass (a)	3 19
Milford		3 29(b)	3 45
Muine Bheag		4 01	4 15
Borris	(3)	4 44	5 05
Ballywilliam	(7)	5 51	6 10
Palace East		6 26(c)	7 25
Chapel	(4)	7 41	7 55
Macmine		pass	8 17
Wexford	(9)	8 45	—

(a) Cross 12.35 a.m. Goods.

(b) Cross B.C. 39.

(c) Cross 5.05 a.m. Goods.

Wexford supply 1 empty each to Macmine, Edermine, Enniscorthy per 6.45 a.m. Goods daily, and replace with 3 off B.C. 40.

B.C. 41.

KINGSBRIDGE TO NORTH WALL AND THENCE TO CARLOW

(Laden)

Commencing date to be advised.

		Arr. p.m.	Dep. p.m.
Kingsbridge (E. and Van)		—	9 45
North Wall	*	10 15	—
North Wall	*	—	11 15
			a.m.
Kingsbridge		11 45	12 45
Kildare		2 18	3 05
Carlow B.S.		4 05 a.m.	—

12.45 a.m. ex Kingsbridge runs Tuesday to Saturday inclusive.

11.15 p.m. Stables at Kingsbridge on Sat. nights and departs for Carlow at 1.0 a.m., Mondays.

B.C. 42.

CARLOW TO KINGSBRIDGE
(Empty)

Commencing date to be advised.

	Arr. p.m.	Dep. p.m.
Carlow B.S.	—	8 15
Kildare	9 24	9 35
Inchicore	10 52	11 00
Kingsbridge	11 15	—

Empty Trucks to be attached to 12 Midnight Transfer ex K'bridge.

GOODS TRAIN ALTERATIONS.

12.35 a.m. Goods, Kilkenny/Kildare.—On and from Friday, 14th October, 1960, and for the duration of the Carlow Beet Campaign, this Goods will run on all week-days, **but on Mondays will leave Kilkenny at 1.15 a.m.**

7.45 a.m. Goods, Kildare/Kilkenny.—On and from Friday, 14th October, 1960, and for duration of Beet Campaign this Goods will operate on **all** week-days.

7.05 p.m. Light D.E. Locomotive, Portlaoise/Inchicore. On and from Wednesday, 19th October, 1960 (commencement date of **Thurles Programme**) this light locomotive will be cancelled. This arrangement will apply until the conclusion of the **Thurles Beet Campaign.**

3.50 a.m. Goods, Kingsbridge/Portlaoise.—On and from Friday, 14th October, 1960, **this Goods will operate from Kingsbridge to Kildare only** and will be worked by steam locomotive of B.C. 35. The Goods will be scheduled to arrive Kildare at 6.40 a.m. **Any traffic offering for stations Portlaoise to Ballyragget should be forwarded by 3.00 a.m. Goods ex Kingsbridge (Tuesdays to Saturdays) and by 12.30 a.m. Thurles Goods on Mondays.**

Ballylinan Goods
  1.10 p.m. ex Kildare ⎫
  4.00 p.m. ex Athy ⎬ Will be cancelled from 14th October, 1960 but will be substituted by Specials B.C. Nos. 35 and 36.

Dublin – Wexford – Rosslare Harbour Train Service Summary (Weekdays)
11 September 1961 – 17 June 1962

	Pass Mail	Pass	Goods	Pass	Goods	Pass	Goods	Pass	Pass	Enniscorthy - Waterford Goods	Pass	Pass	Pass	Goods	Goods
	S*	DT	DE	DE	S	DT	S	DT	DE	DE	DT	DE	DE	DE	DE
	a.m.	a.m.	p.m.	a.m.	p.m.	p.m.	p.m.	p.m.	p.m.	p.m.	p.m.	p.m.	p.m.	p.m.	p.m.
North Wall dep.												From Cork			10.05
Westland Row		7.25		10.15									6.55**	Via North Wexford Line	10.50
Enniscorthy		10.09		p.m. 12.49						5.40			9.35		a.m. 4.57
Macmine Jct.		10.23		1.02						Pass 5.55			9.45	10.10	5.34
Wexford (arr)		10.40		1.22						6.20			10.03	10.40	6.00
Wexford (dep)	6.50	10.54	From Waterford	1.28	12.45	4.05	From Waterford	6.00		7.30	9.30		10.10		
Wexford South	7.06	11.07		1.41	1.15	4.18		6.12		8.00	9.43		Non stop		
Rosslare Strand	7.25	11.19	12.43	1.54	1.32–2.07	4.31	5.08	6.27	7.29	8.24	9.55	Pass 10.13	10.33		
Kilrane Halt	7.33	11.25	12.59	2.00	2.24	4.37	Pass 5.14	6.34	7.35	To	10.01	Pass 10.16	10.39		
Rosslare Hbr arr.	7.40	11.30	1.10	2.05	2.35	4.42	5.25	6.40	7.40	Waterford	10.05	10.20	10.45		

Note (column "Pass DE" from Cork): 'Rosslare Express' Daily until 23rd Sept; then Tues, Thurs & Sats until 4th June 1962. Then reverts to daily.

Rosslare Harbour – Wexford – Dublin Train Service Summary (Weekdays)
11 September 1961 – 17 June 1962

	Pass	Goods	Pass	Pass	Pass	Goods	Pass	Pass	Goods	Pass Mail	Pass	Goods	Pass	Goods	Pass Mail	Goods
	DT**	DE	DE	DE	DE	DE	S*	DT	DE	DE	DT	S	DT	DE	S	DE
	a.m.	a.m.	a.m.	a.m.	a.m.	a.m.	a.m.	a.m.	p.m.	p.m.	p.m.	p.m.	p.m.	p.m.	p.m.	p.m.
Rosslare Hbr dep.	PATH 6.00		6.15	6.40	7.10		8.15	9.20	2.45	3.05	3.20	4.00	4.55	5.55	7.15	
Kilrane Halt			Pass 6.19	6.46	7.16		8.22	9.26	Pass 2.52	3.11	3.26	4.16	5.01	Pass 6.02	7.22	
Rosslare Strand			Pass 6.23	6.52	7.34		8.29	9.32	3.10	3.17	3.32	4.34	5.07	6.30	7.45	
Wexford South				7.05	To Waterford		8.43	9.45	To Waterford Arr. 6.55	3.30	3.45	Pass 4.46	5.24	Pass 6.42	7.59	
Wexford (arr)				7.17			8.55	9.57		3.42	3.57	4.58	5.35	6.55	8.10	
Wexford (dep)	This train operated non-stop Rosslare to Waterford via Campile, arriving 6.57	5.05	'Rosslare Express' Daily until 23rd Sept; then Tues, Thurs & Sats until 4th June 1962. Then reverts to daily.	7.23		7.45		10.00		4.00						8.45
Macmine Jct.				Pass 7.37		Pass 8.08		10.25		4.20						9.50
Enniscorthy		Arr. 5.30 Dep. 6.25 via New Ross to Waterford		7.49		Pass 8.49		10.40		4.33						10.39
Westland Row				10.10				1.30		7.10						Pass 3.43 a.m.
North Wall arr.				To Amiens St. 10.15		9.10		1.35								a.m. 4.00

Key:

'DT' = AEC 2600-series railcars

'DE' = Hauled by diesel locomotive (usually 'A' class)

'S' = Normally steam-hauled, usually by J15 class 0-6-0

At this time, the last few steam locomotives in traffic were eking out their final days in a few isolated places around the CIÉ system. As may be seen in the tables, the South Wexford area still saw occasional use of these, but it should be noted that there was no guarantee that a particular train would be allocated the motive power shown. Substitutions at short notice were by no means unknown, with the unreliable Crossley diesels sometimes rescued by steam locomotives, and vice versa. The Working Time Tables merely showed what was allocated to each service.

Notes:

* This train represented one of the few remaining opportunities by this stage for a passenger to travel in a steam-hauled train

** Left Amiens Street 6.45 p.m.

*** Listed in timetable "Tuesday to Saturday – runs when required". This will probably have been in the event of a late ferry arrival. An operation like this would use whatever rolling stock and locomotive was readily available – steam or diesel.

South Wexford 1978/79 Timetable – Beet and Passenger trains

No.	BS2		BS4		BS6		BS6a		Pass		BS8		Pass	
From	Thurles		Thurles		Thurles				Waterford		Thurles		Limerick	
	arr.	dep.	arr.	dep.	arr.	dep.	arr.	dep.	arr.	dep.	arr.	dep.	arr.	dep.
Waterford		5:35	8:05	9:00	10:35	11:30		15:05		16:40	17:50	18:00		18:47
Campile	6:00	6:17		9:22	11:55	12:20		15:27	16:54	16:55	18:22		19:01	19:02
Ballycullane	6:34	6:49		9:35	12:39	13:15		15:40	17:05	17:06	18:38	19:30	19:12	19:13
Wellington Bridge	7:05	7:55		9:45	13:31	13:40		15:50	17:13	17:15	19:45		19:20	19:23
Duncormick				9:55			16:14		17:30	17:31				
Bridgetown	8:28		10:15	10:35	14:16		16:40	17:45						19:38
Killinick			10:52				18:03							
Rosslare Strand									17:44	17:50			19:50	19:51
Rosslare Mainland									17:56	18:03				19:58
Rosslare Harbour									18:05				20:00	

No.	Pass		BS1		BS3		BS5		Pass		BS5a		BS7	
	arr.	dep.	arr.	dep.	arr.	dep.	arr.	dep.	arr.	dep.	arr.	dep.	arr.	dep.
Rosslare Harbour		7:05								18:40				
Rosslare Mainland	7:07	7:08								18:41				
Rosslare Strand	7:16	7:25							18:48	18:50				
Killinick						11:45								18:28
Bridgetown	7:37	7:38		8:50	12:05	12:40		14:40		19:02	18:47			19:40
Duncormick					13:00	13:20	15:00	15:20			19:58			20:30
Wellington Bridge	7:53	7:54	9:22	9:50	13:38	14:30	15:38	15:55	19:18	19:24	20:20			21:25
Ballycullane	8:01	8:02	10:06	10:21		14:43	16:11	17:10		19:30	20:36	21:11	21:41	22:10
Campile	8:10	8:11	10:40	10:55	15:05	15:35	17:29	19:05		19:37	21:30	22:00	22:29	23:00
Waterford	8:25		11:20	13:05	16:00	16:25	19:30	20:50	19:50	19:55	22:30		23:20	23:55
To			Thurles		Thurles		Thurles		Limerick				Thurles	

Also included in the above programme are the passenger trains. On this section the unusual timetable is designed around the shipping arrivals and departures at Rosslare. There is also a service for commuters going into Waterford in the morning and returning in the evening. It should be noted that at this stage Killinick and Duncormick were closed to passenger traffic. This gives the daytime over to the beet traffic. The daily quotas were Killinick (20), Bridgetown (24), Duncormick (12), Wellington Bridge (31), Ballycullane (28) and Campile (43).

GRADIENT PROFILES

Wexford North

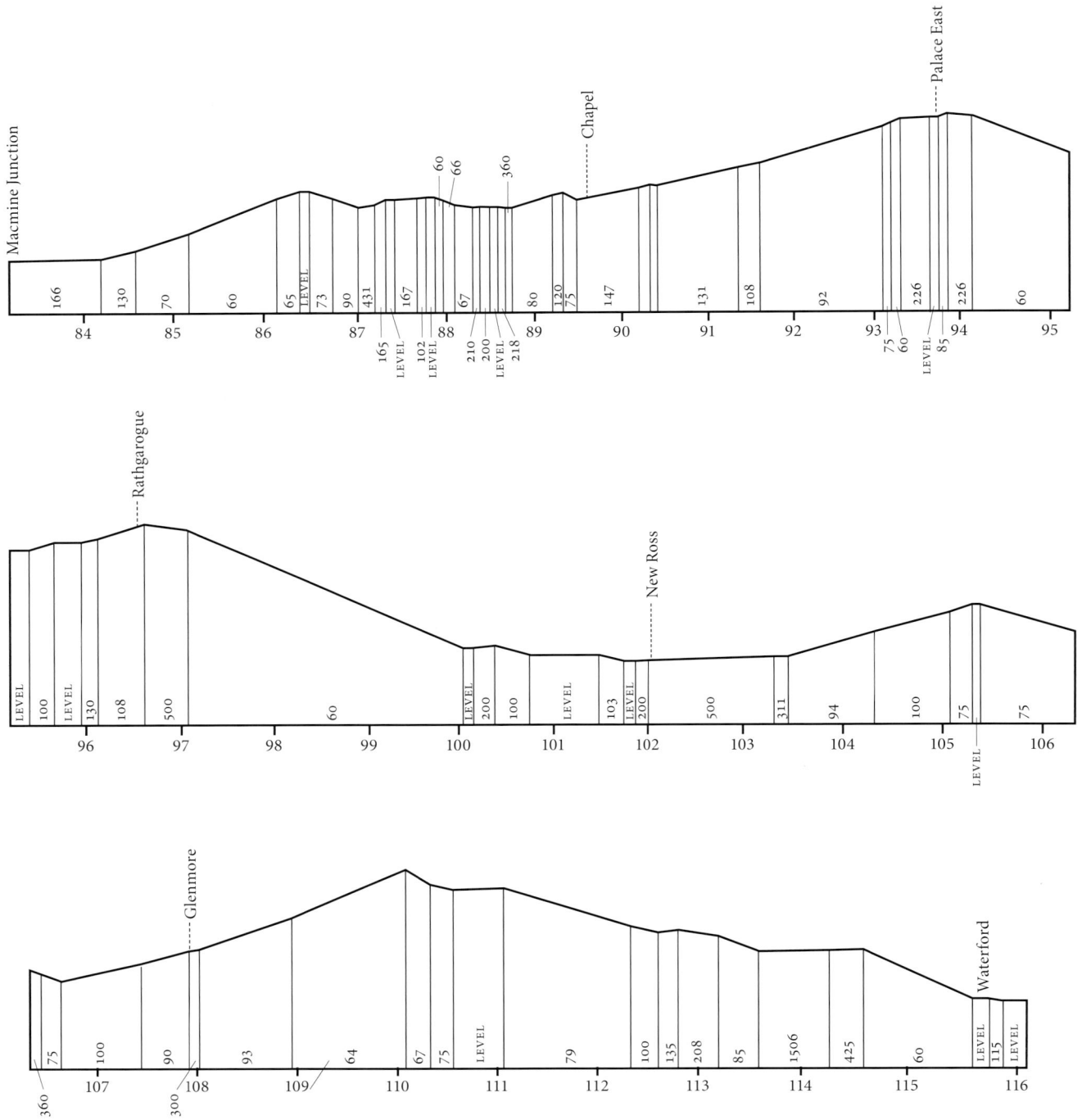

Wexford South

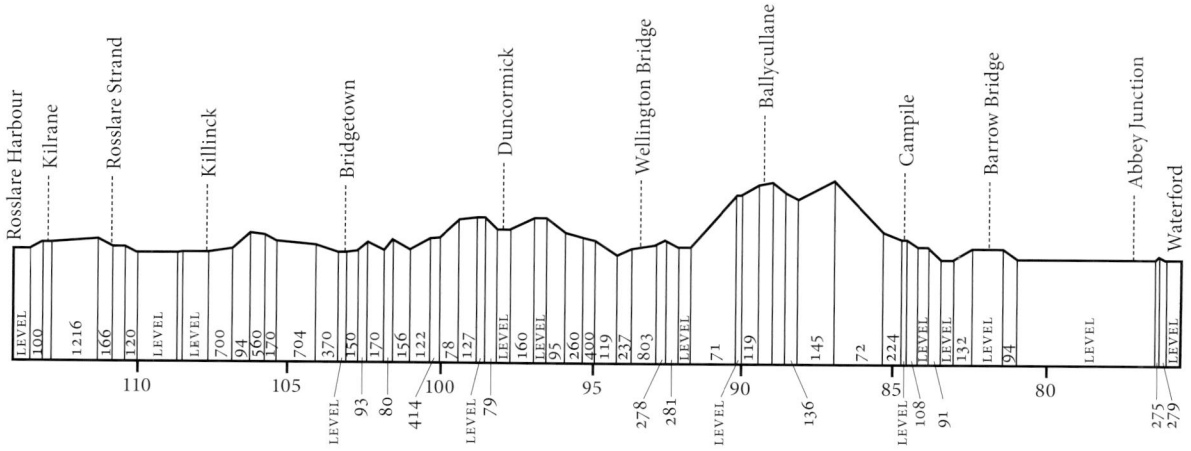

REFERENCES

Throughout the book, references have been made to various organisations which may need explanation:

1. Downpatrick & Co Down Railway (DCDR)

This is a preserved heritage railway based at the town of that name, in Co Down. It was established in the 1980s as a working railway museum and now stretches several kilometres along the former line towards Belfast, which was closed in 1950. Heritage trains are operated by the group, which is entirely voluntary, over this line on selected days and weekends throughout the year. Trains are operated either by steam locomotives or vintage diesel traction, including two locomotives to be seen on the lines mentioned in this book. The railway also has a museum of restored vintage carriages and other exhibits and plays host to the Irish Traction Group. Details may be had at www.downrail.co.uk.

2. Irish Traction Group (ITG)

This is another voluntarily-run body, whose aim is to preserve (ideally in working order) as many different types of vintage diesel locomotive as is practical. They carry out some restoration work at Carrick-on-Suir, Co Tipperary, and other work at Downpatrick, where they have a base on the Downpatrick & Co Down Railway. They also have rescued diesel locomotives stored elsewhere, pending eventual restoration. They operate their working locomotives in conjunction with the DCDR on public trains there. See www.irishtractiongroup.com.

3. Railway Preservation Society of Ireland (RPSI)

The RPSI is an all-Ireland body which was established in 1963 to preserve steam locomotives and carriages in working order for use on main line excursions. Like the organisations above, it is largely managed and operated by volunteers, though in recent years it has taken on paid staff and is registered as a railway operator in the Republic of Ireland.

The Society has its engineering base and railway museum at Whitehead, Co Antrim, a short distance north of Belfast. It has a fleet of steam locomotives, some retained in working order for excursion trains operating out of both Dublin and Belfast, and others as museum exhibits at Whitehead. A replica railway station has been built there also. Details may be found at www.steamtrainsireland.com.

ACKNOWLEDGEMENTS

The authors would like to thank the following, who were of great assistance in the production of this book:

David Carse, for assistance with scanning the images.

The late Norman Campion, for permission to use several of his photographs.

Ciarán Cooney (Irish Railway Record Society) for assistance with several illustrations.

Oliver Doyle, who provided a great amount of very detailed information about railway operations in the vicinity of Rosslare Harbour.

Norman Foster, to whom we are indebted for several photographs of the final steam workings in the area in the early 1960s.

Roger Joanes, for permission to use some of his excellent photographic collection.

Tommy Johnson, for permission to use several of his images of the last workings over the South Wexford line.

Malcolm Johnston and Jackie Hawkes of Colourpoint Press for assistance with diagrams, maps and general production.

Herbert Richards (Irish Railway Record Society) for assistance with research.